W9-ASI-689

Young Howells & John Brown
EPISODES IN A RADICAL EDUCATION

Young Howells & John Brown
EPISODES IN A RADICAL EDUCATION

BY EDWIN H. CADY

OHIO STATE UNIVERSITY PRESS COLUMBUS

Library of Congress Cataloging in Publication Data

Cady, Edwin Harrison.
  Young Howells & John Brown.

  Bibliography: p.
  Includes index.
  1. Howells, William Dean, 1837–1920—Political and social views.
2. Brown, John, 1800–1859. 3. Harpers Ferry (W. Va)—John Brown Raid,
1859. 4. Radicalism in literature. 5. Novelists, American—19th century—
Biography. 6. Abolitionists—United States—Biography. I. Title. II. Title:
Young Howells and John Brown.
PS2037.P6C32   1985   813'.4   85-5013
ISBN 0-8142-0388-4

To Norma Woodard

—one of the little girls who heard
ancient ladies talk of "The Black
String" in the Western Reserve

"OLD BROWN"

Success goes royal-crown'd through time,
  Down all the loud applauding days,
  Purpled in history's silkenest phrase,
And brave with many a poet's rhyme.

While Unsuccess, his peer and mate,
  Sprung from the same heroic race,
  Begotten of the same embrace,
Dies at his brother's palace gate.

The insolent laugh, the blighting sneer,
  The pointing hand of vulgar scorn,
  The thorny path and wreath of thorn,
The many headed's stupid jeer,

Show where he fell. And bye and bye,
  Comes history, in the waning light,
  Her pen nib-worn with lies, to write
The future into infamy.

Ah God! but here and there, there stands
  Along the years, a man to see
  Beneath the victor's bravery
The spots upon the lily hands:

To read the secret will of good,
  (Dead hope, and trodden into earth,)
  That beat the breast of strife for birth.
And died birth-choked, in parent blood.

II

Old Lion! tangled in the net,
  Baffled and spent, and wounded sore,
  Bound, thou who ne'er knew bonds before—
A captive, but a lion yet.

Death kills not. In a later time,
  (Oh! slow but all-accomplishing,)
  Thy shouted name abroad shall ring,
Wherever right makes war sublime.

When in the perfect scheme of God,
  It shall not be a crime for deeds
  To quicken liberating creeds,
And men shall rise where slaves have trod;

Then he, the fearless future Man,
   Shall wash the blood and stain away,
   We fix upon thy name to-day,
Thou hero of the noblest plan.

Oh! patience! Felon of the hour!
   Over thy ghastly gallows tree,
   Shall climb the vine of Liberty,
With ripened fruit and fragrant flower.

                    W. D. Howells, 1859.

CONTENTS

Acknowledgments xi
Prologue 3
Chapter 1: *Becoming Howells* 7
Chapter 2: *Jefferson, Ashtabula County, Ohio* 19
Chapter 3: The Sentinel, *John Brown,*
                     and John Brown's Men 47
Chapter 4: *Poet and Politician* 63
Chapter 5: *From Empire to Eriecreek* 85
Notes 105
References 111
Index 113

ACKNOWLEDGMENTS

ASIDE FROM THE FIRST AND GREATEST, which is recognized in the dedication, many debts accrued for help extended me during the long course of years while the possibility of this book teased at my imagination. It is a pleasure to extend formal thanks to the staffs of libraries: the Ashtabula, Ohio, Public; the Rutherford B. Hayes Memorial; the Miami University, Oxford, Ohio; and the Ohio Historical. The Lilly Library at Indiana University and the Newberry in Chicago. The Library of Congress. The resources, expertise, and good will of the Perkins Library, Duke University.

I owe debts to persons no longer living: Annette Fitch Nelson and Chester A. Lampson, Lyon Richardson, Theodore Richardson, William Hildreth, Albert J. George, and Jack Lunn Mowers. And of course I am indebted to Howells experts like George Arms and William M. Gibson. Thomas Wortham not only rescued me from a bibliographical maze but supplied me with copy. C. Carroll Hollis called my attention to Richard J. Hinton and generously supplied materials. David J. Nordloh and Christof Lohmann opened the resources of the Howells Center, Indiana University at Bloomington, to me. George Arms, Louis J. Budd, K. Kenneth Pye, and John Seelye all read the manuscript and gave me not only useful advice but encouragement to persevere.

As everyone must be who works with Howells, I am, once again, grateful to Professor W. W. Howells for permission to quote from materials that remain under the copyright control of the Heirs of William Dean Howells.

Young Howells & John Brown
EPISODES IN A RADICAL EDUCATION

PROLOGUE

ON 21 APRIL 1860, W. D. HOWELLS wrote a mystifying patch into an apparently commonplace "Sunday letter" from a boy in the big city to his folks back home. In one short paragraph apropos of nothing that went before it, he says: "On Thursday I walked the greater part of the city with a person who brought a letter of introduction from father. I did my duty, I hope; but—" Thus ends the paragraph. The next paragraph lets a short statement stand alone: "Last week I saw Freyer and Sheriff Hendry a few minutes." The following paragraph mentions James Redpath's forthcoming *Echoes of Harper's Ferry*, which is to anthologize young Howells's poetic tribute, "Old Brown," and comments that the poet had declined (he felt too obscure) to let Redpath publish his autograph. All the rest of the letter, like its early pages, devotes itself to chitchat.

What was going on here? A very great deal, of a politically dangerous if not treasonable nature.* It gives us a quick, oblique look at one corner of an episode in the novelist's life, at a key moment in the experience from which he drew nutriment for both his intellectual and creative life. The odds are strong that the Howells family were complicit in John Brown's raid against Harpers Ferry or at least in giving aid and comfort to defeated fugitives who fled to Ashtabula County, Ohio, for safety. They were also involved with such John Brown followers as Redpath, Realf, and Hinton, among others.

Belief in "the Higher Law" and in one's obligation to act in obedience to it no matter what the majority thought had long been familiar to that Howells who in middle age would obey the law himself and stand alone to speak out for the Haymarket Anarchists. It took no exotic influence to turn Howells radical. They thought radically in his father's house, and folks thought radically as a community in Ashtabula County. They planned and acted in the knowledge that guns might be fired, men killed, and other men hang for it. At the risk of complicity in treason against the United States of America with its full practical consequences, they believed that one did what the Higher Law said one must. If necessary, one went conspiratorially underground for the truth's sake — and it was almost certainly about business of that underground sort that father's unnamed friend and Marshal Freyer and Sheriff Hendry had come to see young Howells.[1]

Representatively, Freyer and Hendry made an odd couple. As sheriff of Ashtabula County, Hendry was an early, leading antislavery man and a public favorite at the intense rallies that marked the periodic hangings of John Brown and his men, many of them personally well known to the citizenry. If any man could do a local sheriff's job in the county during those years, it was Hendry. Though most of the senior Howells's editorial venom had been directed against a United States marshall named Johnson, "dirty dog" had become almost a term of endearment for a federal marshal in Ashtabula County in 1860. Hendry "saw" young Howells in a place 200 miles away from his county. Even Freyer may have been out of the strict bounds of his territory. Presumably Hendry went along to encourage Howells to hear Freyer.

What did Freyer say? I think it is a fair guess that Freyer came to stop the sort of game Howells's father had written his letter of introduction to further. Freyer could have said: Ashtabula is out of hand. We admit we can't handle it without troops. We don't think it is worth what it would cost to set it straight. But it's the most isolated county in Ohio. We can keep the Western Reserve sealed off well enough. But we cannot afford to let the same sort of revolt break out down here. Make a wrong move in the Columbus area and we will bring the full force of the laws, state and national, down upon you.

What Howells appears to report home is that he heard and desisted. In the context, however, such an event could only intensify his own radical sentiments.

It has been difficult for literary historians to focus their perceptions accurately upon a radical Howells. He became the writer whose fiction and criticism, whose aid to black authors, and whose action in supporting the creation of the National Association for the Advancement of Colored People won the public praise of W. E. B. DuBois. He became the socialist and essayist whose work drew the approbation of Tolstoi, Elinor Marx Aveling, and the Fabian Socialists. He attracted the friendship of Ernest Crosby and of labor leaders like Samuel Gompers and Morris Hillquit. He sponsored Hamlin Garland, Paul Lawrence Dunbar, Stephen Crane, Abraham Cahan, and Charles W. Chesnutt. He alone stood in a tempest of national fury and demanded that the governor of Illinois commute the unjust death sentences of the Chicago Haymarket Anarchists. He not only wrote to support but he marched to demonstrate his support of the suffragettes. He fought long, openly, sometimes stingingly against the advent of twentieth-century American imperialism.

No one can read Howells's work, comprehend his place in American cultural history, or pretend to assign him a place in American literary history, who has not understood the radical Howells. One good way to begin is to look for root experiences. Many precepts and examples formed him. Deep among them lay the episodes in which John Brown, his men, and the radicals of Ashtabula County, Ohio, all figure. Why, for example, should a man shrink in maturity from the ordeal of

standing up for the Haymarket Anarchists when he remembered men and women who defied the penalties for
treason in order to give aid and comfort to John Brown's
fighters for freedom? Youth and young manhood had
taught him, among other things, to suppose that radical
thought and judgment may be a steady state in an American mind.

CHAPTER ONE

BECOMING HOWELLS

AMILY LEGEND[2] HAS IT that the Howellses were Welshmen possessed of the divine discontent that affected much of Europe between 1750 and 1930. In Wales the Howellses were Quakers and skilled, intelligent folk. Both too low in class status and religiously disqualified for formal education, they were able enough to keep their shops and the water mills in which they wove flannel. They dodged the wage slavery and degradation of the Industrial Revolution. But they dreamed of a New World.

In 1808 Joseph Howells (1783–1858), American patriarch of the family, left The Hay, Wales, to emigrate to America. There was a "Come-Outer" spirit in Joseph that must have yearned for wild, free conditions. He knew industrial secrets about textiles so valuable it was illegal for him to emigrate, and he had in effect to smuggle himself out of England. In the United States, however, he frittered away years and his capital in footling projects until he was free to go West, to the frontier. Perhaps there was nothing else to do. There he cut loose even from radical but intensely disciplined Quakerism. Each in his generation, Joseph's own father and Joseph himself had been "read out of the meeting" for "marrying out of meeting." Each had quietly persevered in attendance at meetings for worship and faithfulness to Quaker codes of dress, speech, and conduct. They were, quietly, doubly alienated—Quakers but not quite.

One can imagine the effects on his family. With baby William in her arms, Ann Thomas Howells had followed

Joseph, deserting everything at The Hay. By the time Joseph was ready for the Cumberland Trail, he was poor enough and William "grown up" enough so the nine-year-old child walked behind the wagon most of the way to Steubenville, Ohio. That frontier town burned with military fever over the War of 1812; and the new boy dressed in defiantly pacifist Quaker garb made a conspicuous target for persecution by establishment boys.

What was William to think when all at once they no longer lived in town but out in the woods? when they were no longer Friends but had a daddy who spent alternate weekends at shouting Methodist camp-meetings? He thought much and tried to think for himself. It seems probable that he emerged not so much in rebellion against conventional, commonplace thought as not really knowing what it was or how it operated.

Perhaps he never quite mastered the conventional. Without taking space to elaborate here, let us say that W. C. Howells spent several years, much of the time in and around Wheeling, Virginia, drinking in, and trying hard to inculcate, fairly extreme forms of deism like Thomas Paine's and democracy like that of Fanny Wright and the Loco-Foco Democrats. He also found the socialism of Robert Owen entrancing. Though there were no few others who held such ideas strung along the ribbon of riverine culture that ran from Pittsburgh around to St. Louis, there were not enough to support a political party or a young printer. In a small fashion, it was the little groups of Quakers, pioneering Abolitionists, who would support tiny papers promoting the antislavery cause. And it was in working for them that W. C. Howells became virtually a founding member of the Anti-Slavery Society of Ohio. They also gave him a chance to learn his printer's trade well enough to earn a living without having served a proper apprenticeship.[3] Such was life on the frontier.

When at last he came down off his Loco-Foco high horse, quite typically he was converted to a sort of contra-diction—Whig politics joined to Swedenborgian religion. Add to that anomaly the facts that he lost neither his devotion to the slave nor his interest in socialism. There were then, and never would be, more than a very few others who lived in quite his world. In ways that count decisively, he would always be "different" in a community and often outside the pale of mutual sympathy or understanding. Paradoxically, therefore, he chose to earn his bread by operating small-town newspapers: and that meant political party journalism, personal journalism, popularity.

II

THE UPSHOT WAS THAT IN 1840 the new editor found himself responsible for the future (including the debts) of the Hamilton, Ohio, *Intelligencer*, the Whig paper in a thriving canal town not far from Cincinnati. With the fantastic "Tippecanoe and Tyler Too" presidential campaign booming along, he could not have found a happier moment. The ruling spirit was enthusiasm—"The Log Cabin and Hard Cider" campaign provided perhaps more fun than Americans ever managed to have out of any other presidential canvass.

William Dean Howells (hereafter "Howells") had been born on 1 March 1837 and was rather young to get full value out of the election of 1840. A *Boy's Town*, 1890, remembers affectionately that there were "always lots of Whig boys" to play with, that they "always had a Whig Club" and the Henry Clay Club of 1844 was a gaudy success. In the boy's town, things went well for his elder brother Joe and him. Apparently they went well for the whole family. Then came aberration and trouble, followed not long after, in 1848, by disaster. In an America moving fatally toward the Civil War, W. C. Howells's peculiar notions could not fail to make him trouble. In an America engaged in forging opposed and mighty principles, his allegiance to Higher Law was likely to bring him to disaster, and in southern Ohio his antislavery convictions were lethal to worldly ambition.

III

BUT IN 1844, HAMILTON was still a pleasant town for a hardworking, well-received Whig newspaper editor. Hamilton bustled with business because of easy access by canal to Cincinnati, turning a good trade in processing pork, flour, beer, and whiskey, in shipping lumber and other forest products south, and in servicing the heavy traffic. Primary Whig principles were business prosperity and national investment to help it; and "lots of the boys" in Hamilton were Whigs. Before 1844 they liked the times and showed their editor their appreciation. "W. C. Howells, Editor and Proprietor" first appeared on the masthead of the *Intelligencer* late in February 1840. A glance at an issue four years later sees the true stigmata of success in journalism: improved format, new types, more, and more lucrative, advertising. Therefore it must have come as a shock to the reader innocent of the editor's complexity to see on 14 May a "Valedictory," announcing the editor's missionary call to religious journalism.

In farewell he besought the Whigs to support him religiously—but his call came from a fearfully odd, little-known sect: Swedenborgianism. The new paper even had an odd name: the *Retina*. Whigs constituted much of most conventional (and probably churched) elements in the population. It is not likely that the fathers of the Whig boys bought many copies of the new religious journal. If those Whig boys' mothers, who must have populated Mary Dean Howells's social life, ever saw the *Retina*, they were doubtless shocked. It bulged with news about communes — and communes, with their reputation for "free love," had no standing among the Whig respectabilities.

Actually, the *Retina* had been published rather quietly out of the *Intelligencer* shop since 1 July 1843. The father's reasons for cashing in his equity in his "political paper" and going for broke with the *Retina* were really false hopes, no doubt encouraged by other optimists. He hoped to spread an intellectual's faith against the serried ranks of evangelical sects. He hoped to establish a significant religious journal on the frontier. He hoped to set up a lens to focus the scattered rays of theological, literary, and political truth abounding in his territory. He hoped to move to Cincinnati and give his powers full scope.

His dreams were idle. Had W. D. Howells never written, there would be little reason to read the *Retina*. As matters stand, it is by far the one best record of the novelist's own religious training. For the rest, the editor simply found much less and less interesting material available than he had expected. Most of the manuscript submitted gave vent to bitter, if not scurrilous, certainly unprintable, Swedenborgian controversy. It would alienate seekers, not convert them. He was reduced to reprinting long extracts from biographical and expository works, even to reprinting Swedenborg himself.

The surprise in the *Retina* became the length of reports from some of the communes then rather numerous in the extended neighborhood. One doubts that the editor, however sympathetic, was nearly so interested in communes as the columns suggest. But he was trying to rally Swedenborgians, and there were many among what Arthur Bestor, Jr.,[4] called "the communitarians." Some ready pens had gravitated to communes, and they contributed good copy. The problem was that they had plenty of words but no cash. Especially in the parallel between Swedenborg's sketch of the spiritual world and Fourier's plan for the social Phalanx was the editor's odd affection for socialism revived.

But his hope came to nothing. His sacrifice was (perhaps necessarily) rejected. The denominational Convention of 1844 voted not to tie the *Retina* (or any similar millstone) around its poverty-stricken neck, and the dreams were dead. By September a humiliated father Howells had charge, under contract, of the "editorial and mechanical departments" of the *Intelligencer*. They took him back, but not to keep. In such a town, it is hard to think that full confidence and acceptance were ever restored, though deep in the savage world of boys perhaps it never much mattered.

The next time around, however, parental disaster would become boyhood's catastrophe, the more because Joe and Will were between them probably carrying the workload of a printer. They belonged to the shop. And because father could run his sort of "family paper" several points closer to the wind than an ordinary employer, his successor lost money on the *Intelligencer* and was glad to sell it back in May of 1845. Perhaps the *Retina* defeat had been recouped. As long, however, as the Howellses stayed in southern Ohio, they could not hope to escape the consequences of betting on reason and peace when conflict and rout swept the world of Ohio politics. Father Howells needed a community that wanted a newspaper devoted to the Higher Law. That would, in Ohio, have to be north of the National Road, probably rather far north and east. Barring his family Quaker connections, which had made him a cradle abolitionist and a charter member of the Anti-Slavery Society of Ohio, father Howells's fate as a political journalist presented an example that was typical of the chaos of the times. In 1844 he felt politically well in tune with the Whigs of Hamilton. By the end of 1848, he had lost the *Intelligencer* again, having led a Free-Soil fight against Zachary Taylor.

The Mexican War, in large, polarized and destroyed the Whig party and the Northern Democrats. The men of conscience streaming out of both parties would form the cadre for the Party of Abraham Lincoln. But southern Ohio held iron-fast to southern sentiments. "Lots of the Whig boys" of Howells's town would grow up to be staunch Peace Democrats—Copperheads. Their fathers in effect ran Howells's father out of town. At age eleven Howells lost his Boy's Town, exiled. His father became a genuine martyr to proslavery politics and prejudice. He lost his shop, business, capital, and goodwill—all but honor. He would have to hustle, scramble, scrounge, do everything a patient, honest man could do, to survive for three years. Then he came back up again, quietly triumphant.

Yet perhaps her loss of status and home securities, anxiety about her brood of little ones, debarment from the middle-class amenities of a woman's life in Hamilton, where a cup of tea turned to a quilting with sociable chat through a pleasant aternoon, hit the mother the hardest. Mary Dean Howells—half Irish and half Pennsylvania Dutch—came back fighting hard. But the stresses she bore were severe. They cost her confidence in her husband's practical judgment. They altered some of her relations to her two oldest boys, gifted, hardworking "good" boys. And of course the adjustment had its own effect, in turn, on the boys, most particularly during adolescence.

IV

FATHER HOWELLS NEVER DRAMATIZED himself or the family, perhaps even slightly, as "victims" or "martyrs" or "sacrifices." His courage and integrity were admirable. But for Howells, almost twelve when they lost the *Intelligencer* and almost fifteen before they were established again in Jefferson, Ohio, the years were dramatic, lit with episodes of real suffering and deprivation, of fantastic experience so strange it seemed almost mystical or neurotic, of the central educational, psychological, affective experiences proper to adolescence. In a sense the move from Hamilton to Jefferson was to be a journey with three stages, and in two of them events occurred that eventually came to be of prime significance to the radical Howells.

After casting uselessly about for a few months in Hamilton, the father concluded a sort of truce and became a "Conscience Whig." That might have done well enough in Onondaga County, New York, but it went for nothing around Hamilton. Finally he found a paper bewildered among changing roles farther up the canal and bought the Dayton *Transcript* for a little down and large promises. As might have been expected, he had bought an unsound horse; and he tried to make him run by working him doubly hard. He and his boys tried together as hard as men could; *they* were the horse that worked. To cover all the markets, they tried putting out a weekly, a triweekly, and a daily every day but Sunday. Howells learned how much defeated overwork hurts.

A morning paper has to be printed the night before.

When Dayton could supply gaslight, father saved money on the piping; and the shop reeked of fumes while Howells set up news off the latest telegraphic dispatches until eleven. Then they woke him at dawn to get out on the streets and carry papers. But he knew that Joe and their father stayed up later and waked earlier before they all began the long day in the shop. At the time Howells did not know how to think sociologically. He loved his family, was loved and knew it, knew they were in trouble and did what was asked of him. But, writing autobiographically more than sixty years later, the well-known socialist commented: "When I think of it, and of the widespread, never-ending struggle for life which it was and is the type of, I cannot but abhor the economic conditions which we still suppose an essential of civilization."[5]

The second stop on the trail to Jefferson often seems, on reflection, like an episode from young Howells's literary passion *Don Quixote*. Howells tried to tell that story for its "poetry" (and for its potentialities of profound self-revelation, I suspect). He tried repeatedly but never quite succeeded. He managed, on the page, to keep his narrative face and voice straight and not give away his sense of how funny and pathetic, how profound and poetic, it really was. The reader has to sense those things upon mature deliberation. But that phenomenon marked much of Howells's finest art. His reader must harvest unaided the growth of emotion recollected in tranquility. What he never could do with these materials was to imagine adequate dramatic substance for his characters.

Father's way of telling the boys that they had lost everything was to come home and burst into the shop in the middle of a hot afternoon with an invitation: "Come on boys! Let's go swimming." Presumably he could get no extension, no new loan to keep the paper. There was no need to set another em for the Dayton *Transcript*. Thus a brave man of faith accepts catastrophe.

But what was he to do now for the lives, including his own, represented by the nine pairs of feet regularly under his table? He had two brothers in Dayton, one of them a prosperous druggist. They consulted, with the spirit of Joseph their father strong upon them, and decided on a Utopian experiment. The world about them stood in dire need of radical redemption (exactly how programmatic they became is not clear). One or both of two great rocks had split many a commune before it was fairly under weigh: the lack of practical preparation and survival competencies; quarrels (as at Robert Owen's New Harmony) ideological and egotistical. They knew they would not quarrel; they were brothers who had arrived at good terms with one another many years before; and they felt competent. With two older brothers (perhaps Joseph and Thomas) to join them later, they would have a real family commune.

Israel, the druggist, could afford to subsidize the beginnings. William and his tribe of willing workers had nothing but time and life to invest; but they were at liberty to start. At Eureka Mills, between Dayton and Xenia, they found land. On it were a working, water-powered gristmill, which could be converted for power looms as in Wales, and a rather ratty old log cabin. A new house must be built. Out to Eureka they went, the children joyous at liberation into the country, the father fortified by hope and faith, the mother almost in despair.

If the *Retina* and hours of shop discussions had not familiarized Howells with the Utopian idea, his education was completed at Eureka Mills. The experience taught him to understand and respect communitarian ideals, but it also taught him sharp ambivalences. Actual

Utopia was for Howells a school of conflict and irony. Not only did it not work (Israel, who was fated to die young, was in poor health and saw that he could never come), the family situation tore the adolescent Howells severely. He loved the brave, sunny father who now had time to make friends and confide in his son that it was right and necessary for the youth to recognize that he was "different" and had a duty to cultivate his literary gifts. He loved the defeated mother, enduring in deprivation and disgrace the primitive circumstances, quietly hating Utopia and bitterly waiting for its failure and the chance to return to civilization and respect.

Though, as his autobiographies show, Howells found the experiences at Eureka so intense they filled a great deal of psychological time for him, Mary Dean had not really long to wait. They went out to Eureka Mills late in October 1850, and they left to go to Columbus late in the fall of 1851. The Conscience Whigs had normal political consciences, and Ohio was producing ever more puissant antislavery political leaders. Statewide their power was growing. In Cincinnati alone, Rutherford B. Hayes and Salmon P. Chase were rising. Father Howells found someone with both sympathy and a job to fill. They placed him as legislative reporter (a newspaper job) with the *Ohio State Journal*. Policy on the paper and father's convictions meshed nicely. Though it was a temporary place, good only until adjournment, it suited the needs of a man who was looking for a good antislavery newspaper. Father, with his personality and his history, must have come to know at least every Conscience Whig, Free-Soiler, or friend of antislavery politics in the legislature.

Of course the word passed that here was an ideal editor for the right sort of paper. As it happened, there was need of one in Ashtabula County, up in the Western

Reserve — if not the hottest, most turbulently abolitionist section of the country, then certainly competitive for the lead. When the men from Ashtabula dealt with William Cooper Howells for his editorship and eventual ownership of the *Ashtabula Sentinel*, he found that he had arrived at last. Ideologically, politically, and therefore economically, he had found his ecological niche in American life. He would become a power in the politics of the state during the "Ohio Period" in the national life. It was a saving step up from failure at Eureka Mills. By the time the family reached Jefferson, however, Howells had seen and suffered for himself something of each of several crucial and modern experiences: what it means to sacrifice prosperity or even one's livelihood for a principle; what bitter toil and fatigue mean when they end, as for most people they do, in defeat; the communitarian dream and its ironies; what it is to be a common wage earner in an ordinary town. He never forgot. He never stopped fighting his own way out. His normal casts of mind were democratic and radical.

CHAPTER TWO

JEFFERSON, ASHTABULA COUNTY, OHIO

HE WESTERN RESERVE, now much compromised by urban sprawl, was long a distinctive American section. Its differences were mainly the products of the peculiar history that accounted for its name. Its population tended to show special characteristics. Politically, the existence of "The Connecticut Reserve" represented the net sum of a series of compromises and concessions over the claims of ill-defined, inaccurately mapped "Western lands" referred to in the colonial charters of Virginia, Massachusetts, Connecticut, and New York. The claims were huge (if anybody had known the true extent of the West and if the present continental United States had been owned by what the states geographically became after the Louisiana Purchase and the Mexican War). Worse still, the areas claimed often overlapped and tangled. It was the great triumph of the government under the Articles of Confederation to compromise those claims, establish the Territorial Ordinances effectively, and create the first template territory, Ohio, which would become the first admitted to statehood.

Politically the Western Reserve existed as a device that cracked hard nuts of conflict. It ceded a strip of land containing 3 million acres, running from the western border of Pennsylvania along the shores of Lake Erie for 120 miles, and lying between 41 degrees and 42 degrees two minutes of latitude. In itself it made a tidy little state in extent and resources. Connecticut used one tract to compensate people for their losses to the British fleet (burning towns) or other Revolutionary casualties. The rest it sold to a land company.

Geographically, the situation was attractive to the pioneering Yankee entrepreneur. He was not the sort that Lowell called "white-pine Yankees"—gentle if gallant, adventurous but bookish, morally sensitive. Yankee pioneers were the woodsy half-savages of the long, tough New England frontier: axmen and lumberjacks, hunters and fishermen, fighters of the short summers, the long, deep-frozen winters, the thin, stony soil. Famously shrewd, hardheaded, argumentative, independent, they were men the Reverend Dr. Timothy Dwight worried about. They might let slip their grip on the heritage of Christian civilization according to the New England way. "Pitch-pine Yankees," those, said Lowell.

They tended to come out of the forests of western Connecticut, the Berkshires, the White and the Green mountains: Appalachian frontiersmen, Yankee style. Geologically their path to the Western Reserve had long since been made straight for them by events of the glacial ages. Once out of their own woods, they had the famous "water level route" of the Mohawk Valley to take them up gentle grades and then the relative ease of cruising down Lake Erie to the Reserve. The land there was heavily forested and would take a generation or so to get drained of its primeval swamp waters. They knew how to exploit forest products, and all before them lay the riches of lake fisheries and commerce. They set to work.

I

PERHAPS NO BETTER EXAMPLE EXISTS of the man of Ashtabula than the local folk-hero for whom the

Sentinel existed. The paper was, to every reader's mind, "the voice of Giddings." From an idealistic point of view, Giddings presented that perfect product of the frontier, "the pioneer." He illustrated the new man, the American, the West, and the future. In the pitch-pine democracy of the Reserve, the Honorable Joshua R. Giddings became, much more affectionately, "Old Gid."

Born in the previous century (1785), he had grown up homesteading on the pure frontier of the forested Western Reserve. He had gone soldiering in the War of 1812. He had seen the elephant and survived. Further, he was, even on the frontier, a notable athlete, built like a professional football linebacker of our day. He stood six feet two (a commanding height for the times), carried a massive musculature, yet kept his agility and fine coordination. Even after the Howellses came to Jefferson, "Old Gid" would return from an embattled session of Congress, kick off his boots, and play baseball on the Jefferson Commons. Afraid of nobody, his mind as good as his body, he kept the common touch—one of "the boys" at home but the friend, ally, and spiritual heir of John Quincy Adams in the House of Representatives.

Giddings not only served the district for 21 years, he owned it. Censured by the House in 1842 for an ingenious maneuver to break the gag rule forbidding debate on slavery, he resigned, came home to ovations and an immediate special election, and was back in his seat five weeks after the censure. Courage kept him alert and adroit in debate. Mass hostility he ignored. Threats of physical violence he stared down, and nobody ever swung the raised fist or stick, nobody drew the Bowie knife or the pistol he had laid his hand on. Giddings said what he pleased through the most fateful and terrible years of the Republic, and what he said pleased "Old

Ashtabula" just right. Other parts of the Reserve had
Oberlin College or the Hudson Academy. They had
Giddings.

Nothing in the mix of Giddings's personality resem-
bled the implacability of Wade or the measureless egotism of Chase. Giddings was, as they say, all man, all
heart. There was that in his warm masculinity which
could not have failed to call out an equal humanity from
father Howells. He too believed in the cause, he could
feel at home in the enterprise and loyal to the man with
whose "Voice" the *Sentinel* spoke to subscribers who
were among Giddings's constituents. Often the *Sentinel*
carried in its columns a "Letter from Washington," sometimes signed G. That was actually the voice of Giddings,
because he remained the corresponding editor.

One of the most interesting things Giddings did was to
forge strong links between Free-Soil Massachusetts
(where they really knew few westerners) and the antislavery groups of the West, where everybody knew and
trusted "Old Gid." His first connection on coming to
Congress he created by moving at once to support ancient John Quincy Adams and his unrelenting war upon
the gag rule. He soon became the comrade-in-arms, and
eventually the heir, of Adams's long-unfriended battle
for a fundamental civil right. The friendship went so far
that Adams, an intensely self-contained old man for all
that he had been the first Boylston professor of rhetoric
at Harvard, wrote in Giddings's autograph album the
following:

TO JOSHUA R. GIDDINGS
Of Jefferson, Ashtabula Co., Ohio

When first together here we meet,
    Askance each other we behold,
The bitter mingling with the sweet,
    The warm attempered by the cold.

We seek with searching ken to find
    A soul congenial to our own;
For mind, in sympathy with mind,
    Instinctive dreads to walk alone.

And here, from regions wide apart,
    We came, our purpose to pursue,
Each with a warm and honest heart,
    Each with a spirit firm and true.

Intent, with anxious aim to learn,
    Each other's character we scan,
And soon the difference discern
    Between the fair and faithless man.

And here, with scrutinizing eye,
    A kindred soul with mine to see,
And longing bosom to descry,
    I sought, and found at last—in thee.

Farewell, my friend! and if once more
    We meet within this hall again,
Be ours the blessing to restore
    Our country's and the *rights of men*.

> John Quincy Adams,
> *Of Quincy, Massachusetts.*

H. R. U. S., Washington, 17 June, 1844,
Anniversary of the Battle of Bunker Hill.[1]

When the hour struck to organize the Free-Soil party, it was to Giddings they looked from Massachusetts to find the indispensable western ally of Palfrey, Sumner, and Charles Francis Adams. His popularity on the Free-Soil side was immense. That did not, however, leave him without political rivals even on the antislavery side in Ohio. Wade and Chase were Giddings's ideological and public allies. Though Wade had been honored with a law partnership with Giddings early in Wade's career, Wade and Chase were Giddings's envious young rivals and competitors, not his friends. Chase vacillated long between the Liberty party and an anomalous Democratic connection. Wade grimly rode his Conscience

Whig party to its bitter end despite the beliefs in the rights of labor and in feminism that made him really the most radical of the Buckeye State antislavery champions. When Wade and Chase had finally to come, growling, into the Republican party, they found Giddings there, already a paladin. The one clear advantage both held over "Old Gid" was youth. He was peaking out; they were rising toward the immense powers they would wield during the oncoming war. His superb health beginning to crumble at age seventy-five, Giddings would not seriously run for office in 1860, and the new age swept past him.

It cannot be easy to feel sure about the qualities of Giddings's mind. The faces he turned to the world— good old boy, high-minded man of faith and conviction, bold though naturally friendly fighter—would serve a politician well in any age. There is every reason, however, to think that in Giddings they presented a triumph of character. Converted to the antislavery cause by Theodore Weld, Giddings found that simple, solid faiths wore well. Yet nobody in the Congress out-worked, out-prepared him. He understood John C. Calhoun well enough to see where the ultimately fatal flaw exposed itself in the proslavery argument of the Old South. He was ready and deft in debate or repartee. Certain excellent minds prefer the simplicity of a few yet sufficient principles they can believe to be unassailable. Perhaps their mode of operation filiates most strongly with those of thinkers like William of Occam.

II

IN THE WESTERN RESERVE, Howells endured an adolescence worse than usually painful. He suffered the humiliations usual to a gifted youth pent in a village.

And Jefferson stood much nearer its frontier origins than to civilized amenities. His identity crises were compounded by sure knowledge of how dangerous it would be to confess his one ambition: to become a great man of letters. His family, in religion and background, was at best strange; and "The Country Printer," as he later wrote in a fine sketch, struck the average citizen with vaguely superstitious qualms.

At home there remained the tensions inherited from the family disasters in Hamilton, Dayton, and Eureka Mills, the stresses of a grim drive to retrieve respectability from debt and the specter of poverty. Even when a syndicate of local farmers volunteered to pay Will's expenses at Harvard, the economic value of his work could not be spared from the printshop. The best chance at education he could be offered was late afternoons and evenings free (after a day's stint at typesetting) to study languages and literature by himself.

As he was always to suppose, excess stress threw him into extended periods of what rather sound like migraines: vertigo, splitting headaches, defective vision. He was haunted for a considerable period by an irrational terror of imminent hydrophobia. Of course, he also suffered from depression. His father, a good amateur physician of the soul, persuaded Will that it was all "hypochondria." Will would call it, self-deprecatingly, "my hypo" for years. It did not disappear until his happy marriage in 1862 (after almost a decade). He suffered the worst of it in Jefferson, and so he came to hate Jefferson cordially.

All those were reasons why Will seems never to have felt much attraction to that good old ball-playing boy "Old Gid." For a time, however, he let himself hope that the other village great man might offer him a means of escape from the shop and eventually the town. Benjamin F. Wade had not been in the United States Senate nearly so long as Giddings in the House, but Wade was a power among the antislavery forces in the Senate. A true pitch-pine Yankee, he had been born in western Massachusetts on a hardscrabble farm and had been brought as a boy to the swamps and forests of Andover Township to grow up pioneering. He was tall, dark, powerful, and a dead-shot with a rifle. He was notorious for invective that was often "coarse" (i.e., he cussed freely). Nevertheless, no firebrand challenged him to a duel either.

In the Western Reserve, they cherish folk-say stories about Ben Wade's putting down "the chivalry." One I have not found in print dated from the Kansas debates:

"Mr. Chairman," quoth a southern senator, "all Kansas needs to become a natural paradise is water and good society."

Wade leaped to his feet to thunder, "That's all Hell needs."

Another Wade retort is much quoted. One southern orator chose to wax sentimental. Should a proposed law excluding slavery from Kansas be passed, he complained, it would "not allow me to take my old mammy with me to Kansas; she on whose breast my infancy was cradled, who watched over my childhood and takes pride in my manhood."

Wade explained icily: "Yes, we will permit you to take your old mammy to Kansas, but we will prohibit you, by law, from selling her after you get her there."

Wade lived in Jefferson and kept the traditional separate lawyer's office in a building a hundred or so feet away from domestic eyes and ears. One of his nephews (perhaps Decius, who became a famous jurist in Montana) was "reading" law in Wade's office. It seemed an attractive proposition to both Will Howells and his family that Will should read law too and qualify for practice. For Will it looked like a way into a profession and out of the shop and village. To his family the cash earnings of a successful lawyer looked better than the unpaid labor of an unhappy youth. Will settled down for about a month to read Blackstone in Wade's office. The nephew and he were to keep up morale by examining one another when Wade was gone.

Like many an author before and since, Howells found Blackstone gritty going. He also found with dismay that Blackstone had loved literature himself but abandoned it because, after a day at Blackstone, he could do nothing literary at home. Eventually, full of humiliation, he retreated to the printshop, the beloved closet study under the stairs, and "hypo." He could do no other. Literature was his one aim and passion.

In two autobiographical accounts of his flyer at Blackstone, Howells was later to be scrupulously fair. Wade was never "coarse," never anything but courteous; but he had the crack trial lawyer's skill in eliciting truth. One day he took up Blackstone with young Howells—and found a reluctant, stumbling student. Tactfully, Wade changed the subject to the five great English literary reviews (the *Edinburgh*, the *Westminster*, the *North British*, *Blackwood's Quarterly*, and the *London Quarterly*) upon which Howells was forming himself for criticism and which Wade read, too. Now he had an eager, lively, knowledgeable student. Apparently Wade said nothing. He just let the lesson sink in, and Howells eventually resigned of his own motion.

Howells autobiographically tried to be precise about his condition. In those years, he said in *My Literary Passions*, "the love of literature, and the hope of doing something in it, . . . was the great reality, and all the other things were as shadows. I was living in a time of high political tumult, and I certainly cared very much for the question of slavery which was then filling the minds of men; I felt deeply the shame and wrong of our Fugitive Slave Law; I was stirred by the news from Kansas, where the great struggle between the two great principles in our nationality was beginning in bloodshed; but I cannot pretend that any of these things were more than ripples on the surface of my intense and profound interest in literature" (Library Edition, pp. 91–92).

Nothing about the coming impact on him of John Brown was fundamentally to change Howells's ambition. John Brown—"as an idea"—taught Howells fundamental, permanent lessons about literature and the rest of his life.

III

WHEN JOHN BROWN CAME TO JEFFERSON to see Giddings, Brown had to break into the baseball game. The spare, leathery man looked like a preacher, but (as seems easier to understand in 1984 than ever before) he was really a terrorist. Perhaps he himself did not know what he was until he sat, brooding silently in Harpers Ferry during the last, long morning before the last road out to the mountains was closed by his psychologically shocked enemy. The man who came off the diamond was an "Honorable" in disguise, a politician who had made a career of candor.

We know that John Brown was not what he seemed. He was more, by far, than he appeared. Apparently he told Giddings on the ball field that he needed money and wished to lecture, and he appealed to Giddings for essential sponsorship. Let the proceedings of the Mason Committee of the U.S. Senate, investigating the Harpers Ferry incident, report Giddings's testimony under oath. The chairman was James Murray Mason, of Virginia; the date was 3 February 1860:

Question.   Will you please to state, sir, your place of residence?

Answer.   Jefferson, Ashtabula County, Ohio, is my residence.

Question.   At one time you represented that district in the House of Representatives?

Answer.   I represented that district in the House of Representatives for twenty-one years.

Question.   Will you please to say whether you were acquainted with John Brown, who was recently executed under the laws of Virginia for offenses against the State?

Answer.   I saw John Brown on Saturday afternoon — I cannot give the date — in the spring or summer last past. He appeared on the ground, where several gentlemen were engaged in playing ball, with a proposition to lecture in our village the next day.

Question.   Where was that?

Answer.   In the village in which I lived. He appeared there for the purpose of making arrangements for his lecture. I was called aside to consult with our friends, for the purpose of making arrangements for the lecture, and introduced to Mr. Brown. This was the first time I saw him.

The CHAIRMAN. I did not hear the date distinctly of that.

Answer.   I cannot give the date. It must have been in May or June last, I think. As I say, I was introduced to him for that purpose, and was consulted in regard to making arrangements for his lecture. I said at once, let him come and lecture. I did not like the idea of undertaking to say, in dollars and cents, what we would give Mr. Brown. My proposition was adopted. I did not leave playing ball, probably more than three or four minutes. He left, appeared the next day, and lectured in the church where I worship. After the lecture, I made an appeal to the people present, stating Mr. Brown's past sufferings in Kansas; his trials and the persecutions to which he had been subjected there; that he was now without any regular employment on which to depend for a living; and for my own part, I was willing to contribute. Our friends generally contributed. The sum I cannot state, but I think it was satisfactory to all. It was less than twenty dollars; it was over ten, I should think. After this was done, I invited him to my house to tea. He took tea with me and with my family, and, I think, one or two other gentlemen. We conversed from a half to three quarters of an hour after tea, in the common sitting room of my residence, when suddenly his carriage drove up to the door and he left me. I never saw Mr. Brown at any other time or at any other place. That was the extent of my acquaintance with him.

Question.

Mr. Giddings, will you look at this note? Probably it may refresh your recollection as to time [Exhibiting the following letter] :

Jefferson, Ohio, May 26, 1859
My Dear Sir: I shall be absent during next week, and hope to be at home during the summer. Shall be happy to see you at my house.
Very truly, J. R. GIDDINGS
[John Brown, Esq.]

Answer.

It corresponds very near to the date which I had stated.

Question.

I wanted to know if that was the period you referred to?

Answer.

It would not fix the time of his appearance at Jefferson or of his lecture. It fixes the time at which I solicited him to come there, but the date of his being there would probably be within three weeks from that time. This I state entirely without any date, with nothing but an impression as to the time.

Question.

Do I understand that that was a note inviting him to come to the village where you lived?

Answer.

Yes, sir. Mr. Brown was regarded as a man of some considerable distinction, or notoriety, if you please. He had lectured in the surrounding villages, except the seat of justice of our county. Perhaps I go too far in saying almost all the surrounding country. He had in a portion of it at all events. Our people were anxious to hear him, and his son, who was said at that time to reside in the town of Andover, had intelligence of this, and the first time I had any encouragement to invite Mr. Brown was on the receipt of a letter from him, saying that he would be in Andover at some time, but the time I cannot fix. In the letter he wrote, I should think he expressed a willingness to lecture for us. The note now presented me was written to say that I hoped to see him at that time, &c., as it now reads. In pursuance of this he called, but the date I cannot fix. The date of his note corresponds with my impression very well as to the time it was written, but not as to the period he was there.

Question.

You say he had been lecturing in most of the adjacent villages?

Answer.

No. He had lectured at Cleveland, at Painesville, and in those places which would correspond in point of population to ours.

Question.

Was the purpose of those lectures, as far as you know, to get contributions of money?

Answer.

I do not know anything of those lectures,

further than what was stated by him in the lecture at our place. I do not know that I ever heard any analysis or description of those delivered in other places.

Question.

Did he say anything in the lecture at your place which would show that the object of his lecturing was to collect money — to get contributions?

Answer.

Not any further than stated. I did understand he was lecturing, and received compensation for it, for the purposes of his support. I got no idea that he lectured for any other purpose but to receive such sums as would sustain himself and family.

Question.

What was the subject of his lecture in your village?

Answer.

Slavery entirely. The duty of Christians in relation to the institution of slavery; the obligations which Christians were under to do to the slaves as they would have the slaves do to them under an exchange of circumstances. In the course of which he spoke of his professions of religion and the religious obligations which we were under to the slaves. He carried that to an extent that we were bound to aid the slaves in escaping, so far as we could, even in the slave States. That was the distinguishing feature in which he differed perhaps from our people.

Question.

Did he develop any plan or purpose, either directly or by intimation of his own purposes, to take measures in any way for the liberation of slaves in the Southern States?

Answer.

From the time of his arrest to the present day I have not only thought and reflected on that, but I have inquired of other gentlemen who heard his lecture, and I am not only authorized to say that I have no

recollection of any such thing, but I have
the word of those who were present to say
that men who were there had no impression of his expressing anything of the
kind. . . .[2]

Giddings's invitation, found among John Brown's papers, and the fact of Brown's having lectured in Jefferson
were matters of public record. They proved nothing not
well known—that Giddings sympathized with the abolitionists. The questioning turned sharply, then, to the
question of "associations." Had there been, were there
now, associations conspiring to overthrow the government of the United States and obliterate the culture of
the Old South by freeing the slaves?

It was a reasonable question. If life in primitive cul-
tures tells us anything about our prehistory, secret societies—cultic, totemic, sexist, ceremonial, and such—are
older than civilization. Indispensable to the American
Revolution had been the Committees of Correspondence, the Minute Men, the Masons. Secret societies,
some of them benign, have always thrived in America.
Not counting the self-protective brotherhoods of slaves
and other blacks, of course the Underground Railroad
had always been necessarily fraternal and secret. Perhaps
one of its strengths was informality—no membership
lists to betray, no internal politics. The real membership
of antislavery societies, counting fellow travelers in tight
situations, must have been, if not larger, different from
what anybody knew.

Of course, that part of the southern imagination which
worried about such matters exaggerated its fears. If the
idea that slaves would rather be free was not thinkable,
then "abolitionists" must be agitating them. Every Yankee became a suspect, and some suffered for it. Some
worriers, mainly Peace Democrats of the North, retal-

iated with their own conspiracy. At its height the Knights of the Golden Circle claimed two hundred thousand members. Posing as radicals, some Knights infiltrated antislavery societies – as the *Ashtabula Sentinel* often complained. It was hard for either side to keep a secret. Even John Brown's plans fell into hostile hands: nobody official believed the secret when it slipped out.

Despite the lengthening historical record, with bales of once private papers in libraries or in print, it is hard to see clearly much about the secret sides of John Brown's rendezvous with history. When they condemned John Brown for treason, papers were burned, mouths closed forever. Gerrit Smith resorted to an insane asylum and emerged able to remember reliably nothing about John Brown. Subsequent and mighty events shifted perspectives; many key witnesses died in the war; evidence became scattered or lost. Contemporaneously, it was, of course, hard if not impossible to get evidence that would stand up in court. The Mason report concludes by complaining of contempt: that "the marshal of the northern district of Ohio" reported that John Brown, Jr., defied the summons of the Senate to appear before the committee. The marshal averred that Brown had armed himself together "with a number of other persons to prevent his arrest," and that nothing but armed conquest of the area could effect his arrest.

Was John Brown, while in Jefferson, "forming societies . . . for the purpose of making contributions" to his cause, Mason asked Giddings, leading gently. Not to his knowledge or recollection, said Giddings. Did Giddings know John Brown, Jr.? From the man's childhood forward but never more than casually. He had once given the younger man three dollars "because he said his father was in want." That phrase "in want" hinted at a Quakerish guile that passed current in Underground Railroad fund-raising. Any Christian must give to alleviate "want" or "need," understood as deprivation, suffering; but a known worker in the cause might also "need," be "in want," of support or travel money for a fugitive slave. It was a Higher Law confidence game. If "A" asked "B" for money because he was "in want" but actually wanted it to pay part of the fare on the North Star Line to Freedom for a fugitive, both "A" and "B" could always testify truly that the transaction was charitable, to alleviate "want." Nothing else had been mentioned.

Giddings went on to tell Senator Mason that "giving money for such purposes was very common" (150). He knew that there were associations for helping fugitive slaves; but, he continued, ". . . I never was a member of any association of the kind. . . . Whatever I have given for the aiding of the fugitive slaves, or for any such purpose, I have always done it openly . . . and have taken pains, at all times, to proclaim it publicly" (151).

It *was* hard to get firm evidence. With all the rest of the smoke eclipsed by that from Harpers Ferry, there had to be plenty of fire. And there was. But how was one to prove it? Clement Vallandigham, the flower of the Chivalry of the Knights of the Golden Circle and a Peace Democrat from Dayton, Ohio, committed something rather too much like an atrocity after the Marines smashed and took the enginehouse at Harpers Ferry. John Brown, old, defeated, was wounded and in shock. Aaron Stevens, so badly wounded it was thought he could not live, writhed in torment. Vallandigham, given the closest chance he would ever get to putting them to the question by *peine fort et dure*, pressed as hard as he could for confessions of conspiracy—and names, above all names—from the Western Reserve. In a "verbatim

JEFFERSON, ASHTABULA COUNTY, OHIO • 36

report" taken on the spot, some of the questioning went as follows, "V." serving for Vallandigham, "B." for John Brown:

V.   "Where did your men come from? Did some of them come from Ohio?"

B.   "Some of them."

V.   "From the Western Reserve? None came from Southern Ohio?"

B.   "Yes, I believe one of them came from below Steubenville, down not far from Wheeling."

V.   "Have you been in Ohio this summer?"

B.   "Yes. . . ."

V.   "When in Cleveland did you attend the Fugitive Slave Law Convention there?"

B.   "No. . . . I was part of the time in Ashtabula County."

V.   "Did you see anything of Joshua R. Giddings there?"

B.   "I did meet him."

V.   "Did you converse with him?"

B.   "I did. I would not tell you, of course, anything that would implicate Mr. Giddings. . . ."

V.   "Will you answer this? Did you talk with Giddings about your expedition here?"

B.   "No, I won't answer that. . . ."[3]

Giddings's name also appeared, and in a hostile light, during the trial of John E. Cook. Uniquely among Brown's men, Cook came of a wealthy, well-connected family and had fought in Kansas, becoming the nearest thing to a *beau sabreur* among Brown's puritans. He had lived like a scapegrace gentleman in and around Harpers Ferry for more than a year, spying out the land for Brown. In a last-ditch effort to save him, his brother-in-law, Governor Willard of Indiana, brought a then famous Hoosier orator, Daniel W. Voorhees, to plead for Cook.

Voorhees's line of argument aimed to show that Cook was just the bad boy of a fine family who had been led by hoary old fanatics and sinners into evil ways. He merited forgiveness, the fate of the prodigal son, not the gallows. The whole John Brown episode, Voorhees declared, vindicated the institution of slavery and left Virginia covered with glory. And, apart from the late John Brown, who were those hoary sinners, the real criminals? Wendell Phillips, for one, and William H. Seward for another. But perhaps worst of all, "an old man, and for long years a member of the National Congress from Ohio. . . . Servile insurrections have forever been on the tongue and lips of Joshua R. Giddings. . . . Shall the old leader escape and the young follower die?" It is said that Voorhees brought tears to the eyes of the jury. But it voted to hang Cook just the same.[4]

IV

VALLANDIGHAM, LIKE MASON, had not imagination to conceive the real pattern of events. Perhaps, in fact, John Brown, though he assembled many of the pieces, did not fully understand it himself. Richard J. Hinton, a member of the band who missed Brown's D-day at Harpers Ferry because he was off recruiting, opined that a federal military movement against the radicals of the Western Reserve could have turned out tens of thousands of armed frontiersmen in defense of freedom. Others had similar impressions. Divide Hinton by ten for hyperbole. Recall that the "embattled farmers" of America have historically been military innocents. Nevertheless the reputed fighting abolitionists of the Western Reserve were a formidable proposition. Nobody took them on. Perhaps, though of course the joke may have been plain and not "Aesopian," an editorial comment in the *Sentinel* for 25 May 1854 (p. 4) signaled the existence of a local band. The editor, a pacifist, wrote: "The days of catching runaway negroes are pretty well over in this part of Ohio. Nothing would delight the boys here, more than to rescue half a dozen or so of them. It would be a very unhealthy exercise for a Kentuckian to visit this country, for fugitives, unless he desired a foot-race, and a good one at that." Howells was then seventeen and, of course, might well have set the type or read the proof.

To understand what the whole John Brown episode, including the aftermath, meant to Ashtabula County and consequently to Howells requires an angle of vision neglected by Brown's biographers. The fighting in some sideshow of a great battle may be of life importance to the soldiers involved but scarcely worth notice to their general. Does the evidence suggest that the Vallandigham brand of nightmare about one, grand, sinister abolitionist conspiracy under Satanic command represented reality? Or do the facts not suggest tens of parochial, locally controlled societies, held together by moral concerns and communicating loosely, if at all? They were "secret" because the laws on one side and threats of violence on the other had forced them into a moral duplicity comparable to that of early Christians in the catacombs. The Mason Committee testimony brought out evidence that Giddings and Brown were not fraternity brothers or conspirators under discipline. They belonged to quite different denominations of the same faith, with wide differences between them in doctrine and practice.

The structures of support that guerilla Captain Brown built for himself and the way he built them suggest looseness and dispersion in his substructure. Moving as he generally did, almost untraceably, Brown came to

Jefferson needing the money he got. But he was looking for other things, and he wanted to see and size up Giddings. He was looking for places and men suitable for revolutionary activity. Given the history of this century, he seems easier to understand than he seemed for perhaps the first two generations after they hanged him. Mostly intuitively, it must have been, he was looking for "safe" areas from which to operate and upon which to retreat and defend if he had to. One of his places was Ashtabula County, and apparently he was liking what he saw.

In times like ours when "information" becomes a sort of atmospheric pollution in the climate of opinion, everybody learns a great deal we would prefer not to know. One such superfluity is a certain knowledge of the modes of operating guerilla and terrorist actions. Rather late in John Brown's life, he discovered in himself a talent for guerilla warfare: Bleeding Kansas schooled him. A talent for informal, dirty war won him coups—the only real success in a life of failure and mistakes.

The Harpers Ferry raid failed not because, given its plan, it was badly done but because a key ingredient in the plan was a dogma common among militant abolitionists: that the slave population of the South was full of men like Frederick Douglass, who only wanted a gun and a chance to battle their way to freedom. That dogma proved to be radically wrong at Harpers Ferry. John Brown captured the guns, but nobody came in to join him and use them. During the last morning when his mistake was patent and one road into the mountains had not yet been closed, Brown's best advisers pleaded with him to be up and away. He sat still and brooded. Did a glint of terrorist genius rise in the captain's mind, or had he long since thought through to that alternative in case of need?

Probably no one will ever know. The question, however, is not whether John Brown was *crazy*: if by the standards of normality not all terrorists are crazy, the word has little usefulness. In our time the world is full of battery-powered terrorists doing nasty little mindless things. But a major terrorist, I should think, sees where an accurate hit, outrageously, unthinkably delivered, will destabilize a major political balance that is already heavily stressed. His hit may have a major, perhaps decisive, effect. With a deal of shrewd calculation and his share of luck, Brown won his terrorist game precisely because his guerilla action failed.

It is self-evident, however, that from the first he did not plan to go into Harpers Ferry and come out a dead martyr. Behind his major plan (to establish a fighting black army in the heart of the South), he laid multiple contingency plans, and that was one of the points at which Ashtabula County entered his picture. Given his youth spent clearing the fields of Hudson, Ohio, of their primeval forests, it was hardly possible for John Brown to conceive of an urban guerilla organization. Working much alone, however, he wove together a wide net of support centers and safe places. Few people and fewer central documents have ever come to light to tell us much about them.

We know, however, that he had brought together a "Secret Six" of believing men, some very rich, centering the group mainly on Boston. It used the Kansas Relief apparatus, often both secretive and confused, for cover; and it raised substantial amounts of money for John Brown. A world away, as worlds went in those days, he had a rural, prosperous Iowa center: Springdale, a community of folk whom the atrocities of Kansas had converted into "Fighting Quakers." Springdale provided, and largely subsidized, a training camp for Brown's men. After the raid they protected Brown's fugitives, defying and defeating the U.S. marshals who came after the fugitives. The main trouble with Springdale was that it was a hard place to reach on the run from Maryland.

The same was true of Chatham, Ontario, Brown's second pillar of support. Wholly populated by escaped slaves and their descendants, Chatham took John Brown in (he already belonged to the citizenry of Gerrit Smith's Afro-American hamlet of North Elba, New York) and largely endorsed his plans, insofar as he revealed them all. Hinton supposed they accepted John Brown into one of the great underground Negro societies. But getting any retreating force back from the South, across the lake, and across the peninsula on which Windsor stands seems unthinkable. If black endorsement was what Brown mainly sought from Chatham, he got it.

There were, however, a number of reasons why he might have preferred Ashtabula County as a base. Still deeply forested in its southern reaches, it was home territory, country a Reserve boy understood. It deserved its fame as one of the hottest, hardest centers of anti-slavery conviction. It was the home district of Giddings and Wade: and, however clean they personally kept their skirt-hems for select committees and all that, it looks as if the county was secretly well organized. On 19 June 1856, the *Sentinel* carried, in heavy type at the head of the lead editorial, a cry to "Friends of Freedom":

> Our country is in danger! Our brethren in Kansas are being stricken down, and ruthlessly murdered by outlaw bands of ruffians, urged on by unrelenting and reckless tyrants, sustained by the army and money of the nation!! . . . Sons of Revolutionary sires, will you come to the rescue? For the consideration of these facts, we invite you to meet in Jefferson, on. . . . the 4th day of July next! Here

renew your vows and light the watch-fires of liberty—take
counsel together and prepare for action, such as emergency
requires!

> W. C. Howells
> C. S. Simonds
> Jonathan Warner, Jr.
> H. C. Tombs
> H. F. Fassett
> Central Committee

Though the later report that the meeting was a great
success covers the *Sentinel's* response to it, apparently
people crowded in, and enthusiasm ran high; if some
such upshot as organization of village chapters of the
Sons of Liberty (or some like name) did not follow, that
would surprise. By 1859 John Brown, Jr., had been per-
manently placed as something like an ordnance officer,
deep down in Andover Township, where stood Benjamin Wade's home place. It was "Brown country," and
from it he could count on almost any kind of help. Every
guerilla leader needs a base where the people are his.
Almost anywhere in the county or the Western Reserve
was "John Brown" country; but he chose a cluster of
three contiguous townships to protect John Brown, Jr.,
too crippled by torture in Kansas to fight, to be the heart
of his base.

The reasons for the choice, personalities aside, were
several. Geography favored it. It might have seemed too
remote to a stranger, with its little crossroads centers and
scattered farms lost in forest. But John Brown knew better. A stranger who came by would be closely ques-
tioned, as a matter of ancient tradition. The first who
inquired about any member of Brown's band would
have heard his news "hollered" from farm to farm on the
old hayseed telegraph. Surprise was nearly impossible.
Better still, close by lay a huge, primeval swamp. It ran
for miles beside Andover and Dorset Townships. Typi-

cally of such, the Pymatuning Swamp was a hunter's or fugitive's paradise, a stranger's nightmare. And Brown's folks had local knowledge.

Nevertheless, perhaps twenty-five miles from Conneaut, with its lakeshore railroad tracks running east and west, its port crowded with Lake Erie shipping that regularly called at Canadian ports, the safe houses at Andover, West Andover, and Dorset gave access to the world. If there should be an advantage in confusing jurisdictions, the border of Pennsylvania ran right through the Pymatuning Swamp. Therefore the area served well for a rear echelon base of operations against Harpers Ferry, a secure place to concentrate munitions or men. If events came to that, it was a potential home base upon which to retreat the army of Negro insurrectionists about whom Brown had dreamed, considering Spartacus. At last, Ashtabula County did become a safe haven for fugitives escaped from the Harpers Ferry disaster.

Though nobody on the Mason Committee could think to ask Giddings about it, Giddings could not have helped "hearing about" the associational work done by John Brown and his men in the Andover triangle during the spring of 1859. He did give Mason a little hint by telling him he had heard Brown was in Andover before they first corresponded. The first mention, little noticed by historians, to a "Black-string band" was written by an anonymous witness and participant, who was, when he wrote, a resident of Andover. It is circumstantial and literate, with a ring of credibility in its prose. It was written some time before 1878, easily within range of a lifespan normal for a man who asserts that he took a direct part in the action.[5]

Given the climate of opinion, it was not hard for John Brown to call to his support (but not his command) men like the Williams witness, who writes:

Early in April, Brown, Kagi, who was Brown's secretary of war, Captain Stevens, and others arrived in West Andover. Brown's Sharp's rifles and other warlike material were shipped to this place, and stored at King & Brother's cabinet-manufactory, on the Creek road, in Cherry Valley. Thence from about the 1st of April, 1859, West Andover became, so to speak, for a time the headquarters for the immortal undertaking of revolutionizing this government by means so out of proportion to the magnitude of the enterprise that most men not acquainted with John Brown believed him to be insane: but to those who knew him, — who knew the depth and fervor of his religious sentiments; his unwavering trust in the Infinite; his strong conviction that he had been selected by God as an instrument in His hands to hasten the overthrow of American slavery, — to such he seemed inspired rather than insane. In a conversation I had with him the day he started for Harper's Ferry, I tried to convince him that his enterprise was hopeless, and that he would only rashly throw away his life. Among other things, he said, "I believe I have been raised up to work for the liberation of the slave, and while the cause will be best advanced by my life I shall be preserved; but when that cause will be best served by my death I shall then be removed."[6]

No distinction, by the way, ought now to be kept between "Andover" and "West Andover." Both in the same township, they were country hamlets, both used postally by John Brown, Jr. Since Cherry Valley Township lies to the west of Andover Township, West Andover was nearer the coffin-factory hideout for Brown's guns, and the son often used the West Andover post office. Personally, he lived most of the time on his farm in Dorset.

During the summer of 1859, John Brown himself fell sorely in want of ready cash to move his munitions to Maryland and ready them for the strike. Alarmed by rumors, his donors were drying up, and he had reason to fear fatal disclosures. He put his best recruiters and money-raisers on the road, including, of course, himself. Meanwhile he concentrated his men in Ashtabula County and found room-and-keep jobs with safe farmers and the like to keep outgo down. It does seem likely that only a rather general conspiracy of true believers in safe country could have kept such matters sufficiently quiet. No wonder Old Gid had heard various things about "associations." Pretty plainly, however, very few even of the most dedicated of the friends of John Brown expected the act of war he launched against the United States Arsenal at Harpers Ferry. Apparently they thought he meant another bold stroke—to attack, free as many slaves as he could, and retreat into a free state. The unexpected thunderclap left them shocked, if not paralyzed, for days.

CHAPTER THREE

THE SENTINEL, JOHN BROWN, AND BROWN'S MEN

*h*OWELLS LIVED IN JEFFERSON until he left home (thereafter to be only a visitor) in November 1858 to work on the *Ohio State Journal* in Columbus. A Radical Republican paper too, the *Journal* served the high ambitions of Salmon P. Chase, the governor of Ohio. But of course Howells went on reading the family paper, the hometown paper, avidly. What would come to him about John Brown's raid on Harpers Ferry?

In point of fact, assuming that John Brown had made a deal with the fates during his long morning's meditation in Harpers Ferry, how and what he won comes through clearly in the pages of the *Ashtabula Sentinel*. The composition starts on a note surprisingly low for "the voice of Giddings." Neither Giddings nor the editor accepted the idea of ending slavery by violence. The paper was slow to accept the factual reports, and on 27 October the editorial pages, condemning everything "the chivalry" had done, added: "We deplore the insane acts of Capt. Brown. . . ." Howells wrote his father (6 November) to protest: "I did hope to see something violent in the Sentinel on the subject of Harper's Ferry." Shrewdly he had caught from Thoreau the substance of John Brown's victory: "Brown has become an idea. . . . I think Brown all the time."[1] Before the month was out, he would write

"Old Brown," a poem sufficiently reprinted and admired to be gathered into James Redpath's *Echoes of Harper's Ferry*.

Meanwhile, in his newspaper the actual "voice of Giddings" spoke. *He* knew when the winds of Higher Law had begun to rise in America. The first page of the *Sentinel* for 10 November carries (where the select, imaginative literature generally stood) an extraordinary "Speech of Mr. Giddings. On the Riot at Harper's Ferry." Its eloquent peroration testifies, at more length than perhaps anywhere else, to his acts in aiding the escape of fugitive slaves. Ill health was retiring "Old Gid." Perhaps this was his valediction to the House in which he had sometimes been a historic figure. He said, for example:

> On another occasion when I was stating the number of fugitive slaves who dined in my house at one time, Mr. Bennet, of Mississippi, publicly inquired if I was not prepared to go one step further? I replied that I was; if a slave catcher had attempted to enter my dwelling to capture those people, I would have stricken him down upon the threshold to my door. . . . If I had the power, I would release every slave on earth before the sun went down. . . .

By the 1 December issue, John Brown dominated, beginning with Howells's poem on "Gerrit Smith." The eighth of December edition, given over to the execution, was a declared "John Brown Issue." Among many other matters it announced "John Brown's Meeting"; and a "Resolution" offered there by father Howells and approved by acclamation, may have marked the beginning of "The Black String." In that "Resolution," W. C. Howells called attention to the fact that, though John Brown had passed to the immortals, he had left "a son . . . in our neighborhood—a noble son of a noble sire—" who has devoted years to "the cause of Freedom" and "suffered not only bonds but chains in our cause in Kansas."

Therefore, with his losses in Kansas, with his resources all poured out for "the cause," we, the "Resolution" proposes, must rightly support our prophets of "Freedom" just as we support our "preachers." The action clause of the "Resolution" suggests that there therefore be a great donation party on 15 December in Dorset.

The idea became so popular that there had to be two parties, one at Giddings's in Jefferson, the other at West Andover. That West Andover donation party dovetails fairly well with the Williams witness and his claim that the "Black String" began in West Andover. In a sense the "donation party" almost exposed John Brown's guerilla center. But just then the chief goal of the federal marshals was to serve the Senate. They mainly sought to bring in Brown's men under indictment before the Mason Committee. From what might have been rapidly forming as a "Black String" point of view, the name of the game was "Fox and Geese."

By 1 February 1860, the *Sentinel* editor thought it politic to dramatize the game. He published both documents of a "Correspondence Between Marshal Johnson and John Brown, Jr." Johnson's ploy was to catch flies with honey. John Brown's testimony before the committee was to give him absolute congressional immunity from prosecution for any crime confessed. Johnson promised to protect him from molestation on his trip to Washington and back: "I will see you safely returned to your home."

Brown's reply is direct, aggressive, logical. To reach Washington, one must pass through either Maryland or Virginia. The first has neither the power nor the inclination to protect one from "the violence of its mobs." Virginia "has especially exhibited of late such a remarkable facility of perpetrating the grossest injustice under the forms of law, that no sane man" would trust himself there. In Brown's own person, he had "experienced too much of slave-holding perfidy" to credit a word they said.

In the second place, under oath he would be compelled to implicate other people, and such a thing, by a solemn oath to God, he would never do: "I cannot purchase immunity from further prosecution by an act of *treachery*." For one thing, many of them are Black and still in the South, still subject to "that system of piracy" we call slavery. He does not plan to flee abroad, but to stay quietly at home — and let U.S. Marshal M. Johnson, Esq., make the most of that.

Perhaps it is right to assign to about late January the legend most often told in Jefferson about W. C. Howells and John Brown, Jr. The story runs that Brown was in the *Sentinel* office talking when someone noticed a U.S. marshal (Johnson? Freyer?) walking toward the door. While Brown slipped out the back way, Father Howells kept him engaged in conversation until Brown was safely on the road back to Dorset — and no doubt safely escorted, too. Conceivably, it was to deliver to the editor the text of his reply to Johnson, and even to discuss its firm style, that Brown had ventured out to Jefferson that day.

John Brown, Jr.'s confidence that he would live quietly at home in Dorset may testify to the fact that the Independent Sons of Liberty, popularly called "Black String," came into being between the 15 December "Donation Party" and 1 February 1860. The man from Andover recorded that "as knowledge of its existence extended new associations or lodges were organized; and as this went on, to insure uniformity of work and harmony of action, an affiliated secret society was formed." A state lodge, and finally a "United States lodge." It aimed to overthrow slavery, politically if possible, "in a revolutionary manner, if necessary. . . ."

On 21 March 1860, the *Sentinel* and the county put on
their biggest, most defiant, but really their last, John
Brown fest. Though the friends of John Brown were
winning their own game, new historic events were rapidly rewriting the rules, changing the game, pushing John
Brown into the historical background. Soon he would be
to all but a faithful few a myth: his soul is marching on.
Perhaps in some fear of that, the editor himself published a letter, virtually unique for him, in the 14 March
1860 issue. He had also called for a great rally in mourn-
ing for the deaths of Hazlett and Stevens, the last of
Brown's men to be hanged, the meeting to be on 16
March, with John, Jr., and Owen Brown, Barclay Coppoc, and James Redpath. Owen Brown and Coppoc
(they also promised Merriam as a bonus) were indicted
fugitives from the raid. Redpath, like the junior Brown,
stood in defiance of a Mason Committee summons. The
Black Strings were their surety now for even public ap-
pearances. But, on the other hand, were the events of
1860 not displacing the John Brown question from the
center of public attention?

Father Howells's letter from Columbus of 4 March,
published in the 14 March issue, sounded tones rare in
the Ashtabula County discussion of John Brown. In a
Goldsmith vein, it describes a lovely spring walk. A
literary note is struck (his companions are "the author of
the 'Poems of Two Friends' "—or least one of them, his
son Will—and the latest English lecture performer, Richard Realf, who was a John Brown enthusiast). Suddenly,
as in a romantic musical suite, a note of thunder rumbles.
Somebody in Ashtabula County, a traitor, has told the
governor of Virginia where he could find Owen Brown!
The reaction, as from father Howells, is furious: "If the
man is known, let him be marked, and treated as he

deserves. If I knew the man, I would make the country too hot to hold him." The moral is that spies lurk about; watch your tongue.

Editor Howells proposed his solution:

> I would like it if Owen Brown, and Merriam, and Tidd, and Coppoc, could feel safe to live in our country because there was not a man mean enough to betray them. But . . . there are houses in abundance where they can receive the hospitalities of the family, with all the sacred observances of those rites of the House that true honor prescribes. . . . We can maintain secrecy; we can frown on, and refuse intercourse with spies; we have houses, and homes, and hearts, to lend refuge; and the fastnesses of the forest that God has given us, as means of public defence.

Should all these fail, it would be time to "discuss other means." In a matter of two days from publication of the foregoing, he proposed to put a number of the refugee guests on public display. He promised to. Had he issued a warning?

At the roaring rally held for Albert Hazlett and Aaron Stevens, Coppoc was present but too acutely asthmatic to speak. Merriam was not there. James Redpath, who tried unsuccessfully to capture the meeting, was eccentric in appearance and manner and too militant to impress. Really what he sought was immediate mass invasion of the South to free the slaves now. Of the regular speakers it was John, Jr., and Owen Brown who made the hits. John, with ready wit, brought down the house in one moment of repartee. His brief biographies and tributes to Stevens and Hazlett went well. Owen came on as a sort of lesser Giddings, a good old boy well-converted who wanted to do right and was ready to fight to destroy evil. They concluded the last rally with a fire of Lincolnian jokes, personal, ego-deflating, yet striking straight to the mark of an idea.

At the *Sentinel* as everywhere, the files now began to be closed on the John Brown case. The 16 March rally turned out to be the last hurrah. In "Old Ashtabula" they did their duty by the fugitives so long as it mattered. But, after Lincoln's nomination, it ceased to matter so much. Freedom, what tragedy had left of it, opened again. After the southern senators had departed, who wished to investigate 1859? The "Black String" was faithful, but of course the Browns moved out of the fort, which had after all been a prison too. Most members of the several societies recalled that they had sworn themselves to silence and held their peace. Certain others, feeling perhaps a duty to get these states stated, get the true history into the books, tried to tell it. And thereby hangs a historio-graphical tale.

I usually think that discussions of the documentary and other reliances for believing (or not) in the probability of the truth of an assertion in history ought to be soundly whipped and confined to their kennels. The case for believing that "the Black String" existed and functioned rests on narrow odds, however. I started wondering curiously, doubted, disbelieved, and doubted again as the evidence trickled in. Now I believe that there was in fact a "Black String," that it performed its sworn function, and that the scenario of facts, taken whole, profoundly influenced Howells. If the tale is worth telling at all, it is worth the space to tell chronologically.

At least until the mid-1920s, old ladies in the Western Reserve reminisced at tea about "the Black String," speaking with such a touch of the aura of secrecy that the little girls playing at their feet picked up the phrase, simply as phrase, and remembered it. There was a folk tradition. And then there is the Ur-document, the anonymous witness of the Williams *History*, writing at a date when a great many of the local participants must have been not only present but lively. The witness writes firmly and authoritatively, as a prime mover, a chief actor, afraid of nothing. He wishes to set down for the first time a "Chapter of History." And he intends to illustrate "the fact" that "no part of the United States was more devoted to human liberty" than Ashtabula County. He wants also "to perpetuate a scrap of unwritten history." Barring his anonymity, no witness could be more convincing.

One of the next generation, snatching at fame and fortune by exploiting the noble past of Old Ashtabula, mingled the scent. Chet Lampson, who began as something like a George Ade character (small-town flash leaps wildly at the big name and the big money), ended up like a Spoon River or *Winesburg, Ohio,* character (failed author, failed historian, mediocre antiquarian, a "grotesque" in costume, manner, and habit of thought). He studied the Western Reserve all his life, but he never quite knew what to do with what he knew. The Ohio Historical Library collections are rich in papers he unearthed. There are three general sources, by no means all agreeing, for Lampson on "the Black String." One was an article he wrote and published in the 8 October 1899 Cleveland *Plain Dealer.* It appears at length in the Sunday Morning Magazine Section as "The 'Black String' Band." The second was conversation, ever varying with the occasion, with Chet. His first nervous fears conquered, he talked in self-associated bursts, and he was never organized or consistent. His writing often showed the same dangers to navigation. A good deal of similar conversation he worked into his personal "column" in the *Jefferson Gazette,* and in 1955 he used the resources of his shop to publish for himself a short volume entitled *John Brown and Ashtabula County.*[2]

Chet Lampson was nevertheless an intelligent, hardworking man who lived out his time and survived in a public relations business among a folk many of whom felt reservations about him. He had talent and courage. What went wrong? A column of 23 June 1942 is revealing:

> When I was a youngster and in my early years as an editor, I wrote a story of the anti-slavery movement in this section, and dug up some well-hidden secrets about the Black Strings and about a real plan to force Ohio to secede from the Union. . . . I wrote the story largely to prove to a certain woman . . . that I had not lost interest in cultural development. I did not make much headway, but I did develop a great story that in years to come may provide you with something of real value.

1900 was near the heyday of the blood-and-thunder and cloak-and-dagger romances. It was that day when, as Howells remarked, you could not hear yourself think for the horrid noise of the swashbucklers swashing upon their bucklers. One fair guess is that Lampson could not readily keep track of details because he confused memory with romantic imagination. Second, he did not know how to order and control information.

For an instance, why did they call them "Black String Bands" or anything such? Why "Black String"? Because, folksay, the Williams witness, and Lampson agree, black string or thread was used as a means of identification. Secret identification needs to be swift, sure, easy to spot, yet safely secret. That seems to debar the notion that identification was established by the member's wife's mixing some black threads with the white when she sewed on her husband's collar-button. A feminine eye might have caught that signal at once, a masculine eye seldom, especially not at random. It would have been a badge too conducive to fatal error. Too obviously, it might seem, a bit of black twine knotted through a button-hole would call attention to its wearers. What if ten farmers should congregate on a corner of the square and find that four have mysterious, miscellaneous bits of string dangling from their coats? Will no one ask a question? If he does, what can one do or say to dodge suspicion, even crisis?

Though it is not in his published writings and may have lived only as one of his romantic notions, an explanation given me once orally by Chet Lampson would seem to make sense of the black string aspect of "The Black String." Every initiate had to carry, he said, a bit of black string of a prescribed length, produce it if challenged, and know the one way to wrap it about one's fingers prescribed for members only. Shall we ever know the right answer? Perhaps—after we have found a copy of the ritual, "the work," as the Williams witness called it.

Although Old Ashtabula held faithful to its mission of protecting the surviving Browns and their party, events moved fast. They might "forget" later than the rest of the nation, but for the time being they kept the faith. Nevertheless, the world moved, and even the Black String could be spoofed. In the *Sentinel*, 13 June 1860, ran a true frontier "sell" of a story. Headlines shouted: "ATTACK ON JOHN BROWN!" and "*Great Excitement in Dorset!!*" It seemed that "a party of a dozen or more" had descended on Dorset. Brown, not able to fire for fear of his household, "received a perfect torrent of *blows*," and "his power of endurance throws Heenan and Sayers in the shade." Finally, "*by some stratagem of Mrs. Brown*," the attack was dispersed. The key to the "sell," for the alert reader, lies first in the weaponry of the assailants— "single-barreled breach-loading brass smoothbores" and in the last remark: "What *Brass* this Andover *Banditti* must have had!" In short, the only attack permitted by the Black String on John Brown, Jr., was delivered by

Their Very Own. They had a sort of shivarree, a concert by the Andover Brass Band to liven him up. A sense of entire security must have descended on them.

The worst crux in the tangled, dubious web of Black String evidence comes in an event I have not been able to locate in the *Sentinel* but which Lampson attributed to Joseph A. Howells, Howells's elder brother, highly successful editor of the *Sentinel*. "Joe," as everybody in the family called him, both flatly and sharply denied that there was any truth to Lampson's *Plain Dealer* piece. Worse, for Lampson to publish it was an attack on the memory of the great deed and a danger to the living. A charge of "treason" has no statute of limitations. Joe denied in general and in particular all credence to Lampson; and, generationally, Joe had been a man on the scene, close to the heart of things, when Chet Lampson was not yet.

I suspect that Joe was less than candid, not ingenuous. He protested too much. Flat denial and rejection of the existence of anything like "Black String Bands" and such leave us with too much to account for from witnesses other than Lampson, including, of course, the fact that Ashtabula County turned out to be a secure place not only for John, Jr., but all of the Brown Party who sought comfort and aid. Somebody provided labor and horses to move munitions about, stored guns, some ingeniously, to make ready for the move on Harpers Ferry, and guarded the operation diligently. And, when it was over, they not only fed and sheltered and protected fugitives but intimidated their pursuers. There is folk-say; there are newspaper stories and scraps of such little history as come out in Williams and Hinton.

That it is almost impossible to prove a negative, Joe Howells was more than wise enough to know. That it seldom happens that a good yarn can be suppressed even by the flattest denial he also doubtless knew. But he tried. Eventually the Howellses would sell the *Sentinel* and the papers be "merged"—with the *Jefferson Gazette* on top. At the time of the *Plain Dealer* article, Lampson was in his jumpy puppy-dog phase of life and as much a nuisance as a rival to the established *Sentinel*, with its nationally known name, its dignity and savvy, and its long prestigious history. Apparently, Joe Howells hit hard at Lampson and his "Black-String" piece. I think he hurt him badly, but he did not knock him, or the issue, out.

Straight in the face of all Lampson's research (oral and documentary and in family lore), Lampson wrote plaintively, "I was amazed by the denial in the Ashtabula Sentinel by J. A. Howells, son of W. C. Howells and brother of the great American author, that any such treasonable organization ever existed in this county" (35). In his defense, Lampson might have been able to make better use of the Williams witness had he used him (whom he later says was Benjamin Perry) fairly from the first. Ah, youth!

There is, finally, almost no probability that if there were "Black String Bands" Joe Howells did not know it. I do not think there is much probability that there were none: the lists of Lampson's witnesses and the reports of what they said jibe too well with the public documentation, such as it is. When Lampson took his grievance to Howells, he got a chuckle and a dismissive: "Oh, well! You know they didn't always tell Brother Joseph everything." Free to make of that what he would, Chet decided to say nothing. He just hung on, essentially, to what his grandfather had told him about the Black String. I am not sure we shall be able to learn more now than we know; strange things happened; stranger things still were adduced to explain what happened—or did not. Perhaps there is a letter buried in some holding.

Suppose Joe in his denial *was* disingenuous? Suppose, somehow obeying the Higher Law, he committed a falsehood that high truth and honor might live uncompromised, not rationalized? That could have happened. What, transcendentalisms aside, could have motivated him? In the first place, Joe had won in the game of life. He had kept his promise to his mother. With labor and shrewdness, knowing how to turn the family knacks for literature and improvisation to account, he had edited, printed, and sold by the thousands for use by McClellan's Army a popular collection of songs in a handy envelope. Innovative, it became a best-seller. The income put the family, which held all its property in Mary Dean's and Joe's names anyhow, in the black for the first time. Joe paid off the notes on the house and the *Sentinel*, and he built a "state of the art" small publishing shop in a new *Ashtabula Sentinel* building. Now at last the family were undeniably "respectable," and Mary Dean could die in the odor of that status she had long feared her husband had sacrificed to the Higher Law forever.

Joe, in due course, became a solid man of affairs in Ashtabula County. With seniority, he became "The Editor": and hearts and fans trembled when he was seen at some affair to take out his pencil and jot down "an item." With the sons of men like Giddings and Wade, he became a power in the ponderously growing Republican party. Though their fathers had founded it, in practical terms they early manned and commanded it, at least in Ashtabula County. Thomas Nast had not yet seen the GOP as an elephant, but the new generation of "boys" in Ashtabula County knew that they fought a war, made a difficult peace, and felt confronted by unprecedented problems. Whether one might be able to exercise power or not rested, democratically, on power to control enough local units and get out the vote on your side.

Solid men counted at just that point. Interspersed with family comment, often charming, Joe enumerated his posts, positions, services, and brokerages of power in a letter requested by a researcher in 1895. In fifty hard years, he had fought his way from printer's devil at the *Intelligencer* to presiding over the board of trustees of a university; and he had stomach ulcers.

One great problem becomes evident as soon as a target so inviting to malice takes shape. If Joe admitted to aiding the Brown party, Joe and other people had no sure defense. Hard as the case would have been, forty years after and out of a district always deadly hostile to the government on such an issue, the defendant's only course (presuming he had helped Owen Brown, or Coppoc or Merriam, or Tidd) would have been the unhappy tactic of not taking the witness stand. With no statute of limitations for treason, or for action accessory to the commission of treason, Chet Lampson's defective sense of time threatened to visit a dirty, sensational, destructive chain of events upon Joe Howells. I think he would have won in a trial, but at some psychic cost. Every advantage would have accrued to Lampson, who (judging by the writing in his *Plain Dealer* piece) was not then likely to have thought matters through. Grant appointed him Jefferson's postmaster in 1866, and altogether he held the job for twenty-one years. In Jefferson he served on the town board of education for twenty years. He stood stalwart in Republican machine politics, chairman of the county Republican central committee for ten years and climbing steadily in the state organization. He also built a career as a supporter of black higher education in Ohio and became a trustee and at last the president of the board of trustees at Wilberforce University.[3]

Second, Joe Howells had to look to his father's reputation. I now think that, abandoning, like many a pietist in the war soon to come, his pacifist conviction, father Howells was silently complicit in the organization and mobilizations of the Harpers Ferry raid and, more than complicit, active in the Black String aftermath. The Black String Bands were accessory to acts of treason by reason of sheltering and protecting the Harpers Ferry fugitives. Of just what they were guilty in giving equal shelter, fortification, and immunity to John Brown, Jr., Redpath, and any other protestants against the Mason Committee, I am not sure. Certainly they were accessories to acts of contempt of the Senate of the United States. And there still lived old friends, of both races, to consider.

Finally, Joe Howells must have been as acutely conscious as anyone alive of what had become of the stand by the embattled farmers of the Pymatuning. Thousands of Confederates had committed acts of slaughterous treason against the United States—and enjoyed mass pardons. But who had pardoned Brown and Brown, Merriam and Coppoc, Tidd—or, more to the point, their surviving friends and other complicit persons? When the Lincoln/Douglas–Breckenridge/Bell campaign began to heat up, John Brown and his people faded from the news like a half moon before a rising sun. They went out of reality into myth, until marching Union troops began to chorus, "John Brown's body lies a-moulderin' in the grave, . . . His soul is marching on." Why? What did it share with "Tipperary" or "Lili Marlene"? Who can say?

At any rate, so far as the Black String was concerned, the whole thing began with a bang and went out on a whisper. What did it *matter* now? Joe could have proved to Lampson from some of Will's best columns that Chet was coming at fiction all wrong. Or Will's novel *The World of Chance* (1893) would have shown him the same thing from another angle. Considering Chet's life, one rather regrets his not having read, marked, and inwardly digested *The World of Chance* before it was too late. Why, then, should John Brown in a neat cameo have dominated the opening section of *A Chance Acquaintance* (1873), Howells's "first true novel," as he said?

CHAPTER FOUR

POET AND POLITICIAN

*i*N THE LAST ANALYSIS, what Giddings, John Brown, and Brown's men taught was an American faith that Lincoln expressed so memorably in his debates with Douglas that his words have entered the national book of secular scriptures. The one true issue between him and Douglas, Lincoln said, lay in Douglas's determination to evade slavery, not to talk about it. What matters, Lincoln said, "is the eternal struggle between these two principles— right and wrong—throughout the world. . . . The one is the common right of humanity, and the other the divine right of kings. It is the same principle in whatever shape it develops itself. It is the same spirit that says 'You toil and earn bread, and I'll eat it'. . . . And whenever we can get rid of the fog which obscures the real question. . . . there will soon be an end of it. . . . There will be no war, no violence."

In descending order from belief that pure commitment to war was the one feasible means of extinguishing slavery, one might place Brown, Giddings, and father Howells. They believed in the mandating force of the Higher Law. Lincoln did not, and Howells was prone in those days to say nothing much about matters religious. He was a Radical Republican but not an extremist of the Redpath, Hinton, or (perhaps) Black String type. Perhaps that was one reason why he got the assignment to write a campaign biography of Lincoln. Meanwhile, his experience of John Brown had sounded a new note in his poetry—a note of radical protest with associated notes of a determined, masculine democracy that his writing would never long forget. The radical mode would peak in *Stops of Various Quills*, 1895; but it would always be there, often speaking in some quick, ironic turn.

Howells learned the printer's trade because he literally grew up in printshops. The shops existed to print newspapers. And it was then the normal condition of a paper to earn its way by selling subscriptions to members of political parties. Take away the band of loyal party members who rallied about their paper and you got the Dayton *Transcript* and ruin. Give the paper common cause with loyal, even fiercely concerned party members and you got the *Sentinel* — prosperity, influence, state or national renown, perhaps even a slice of political patronage.

Though he says so little about it autobiographically that unwary critics have been deceived, young Howells was a political pro. He had grown up with shop talk and family talk about politics in his ears every day. He had searched "the exchanges" — other newspapers — for hot items to use, and he knew how they handled politics. Before he came to a provincial rest in Columbus, he had edited the *Sentinel* in his father's absence, had worked with great success as a legislative reporter for Cincinnati and Cleveland papers, and had tried being city editor of the Cincinnati *Gazette*. On the *Ohio State Journal*, he worked mainly as a "paragrapher," a writer of quick, funny but mordant pieces; and again he worked with the "exchanges" — though with the paragrapher's intent behind his searches. He knew politics and politicians and did not hesitate to claim full professional competency as a political reporter when applying for jobs from the editors of New York newspapers.

His first try at long fiction — in the *Sentinel*, when the author was seventeen — would have been a political novel if it had not broken down: its center of action was a political contest. He would write campaign biographies for Lincoln and Hayes. Political concerns were seldom out of his view. And yet he himself undertook to persuade his readers that he was purely a "literary creature." Why? Because to be an artist, an author, and earn his livelihood that way was almost his supreme ambition. Because, until relatively late in life, his truly highest ambition was literary fame won through artistic mastery. Politics like journalism he came to consider relatively mean. The values behind and beyond behavior, however, he came at last to think absolutely supreme, superior to artistry or fame. To that belief his John Brown experience contributed importantly.

I

YOU CAN HEAR THE DIFFERENCE in even the first of the John Brown poetry, written before John Brown was hanged. Poet and politician have merged in Howells for the first time, and the poet has changed. His pre-Brown poetry is well-represented by that "Andenken" which compelled Lowell to think he must re-read all of Heine's verse to be sure, before he accepted it, that it was not simply a translation. It has 116 lines in six sections as published in the *Atlantic* for 1860; it was too long and Howells later edited it down. But it had some excellent poetry in it. The conclusion, long though it is, is worth quoting:

VI

I remember the burning brushwood,
  Glimmering all day long
Yellow and weak in the sunlight,
  Now leaped up red and strong.

And fired the old dead chestnut,

That all our years had stood,
Gaunt and gray and ghostly,
  Apart from the sombre wood;

And, flushed with sudden summer,
  The leafless boughs on high
Blossomed in dreadful beauty
  Against the darkened sky.

We children sat telling stories,
  And boasting what we should be,
When we were men like our fathers,
  And watched the blazing tree,

That showered its fiery blossoms,
  Like a rain of stars, we said,
Of crimson and azure and purple.
  That night, when I lay in bed,

I could not sleep for seeing,
  With closed eyes to-night,
The tree in its dazzling splendor
  Dropping its blossoms bright;

And old, old dreams of childhood
  Come thronging my weary brain,
Dear foolish beliefs and longings; —
  I doubt, are they real again?

It is nothing, and nothing, and nothing,
  That I either think or see; —
The phantom of dead illusions
  To-night are haunting me.

The central image of the long-girdled and seasoned tree burning all over at once when at last it caught fire was a common frontier sight. Almost surely Howells had seen it and most probably at Eureka Mills. Throughout the poem come moments which suggest that in inspiration "Andenken" was a considerably Oedipal poem. But Freud was still a child when the poem was composed, so the poet worked naïvely.

But who in the United States of 1859 and of Howells's generation was writing poetry as good as the best of

"Andenken"? Howells had hammered himself into an accomplished Heinesque-American poet. The very process and product, however, illustrated what Howells the mature realist, critic, and theorist would roundly damn as *literose*. Literosity was the deadly sin of producing literature only out of other literature, never looking to common human life for inspiration or authority. Literosity could be perfectly instanced from Howells the Heinesque. Until the real world began to break through his ever so painfully cultivated Heineism, he would be literose, his work would be mere literosity. The real world began to break through in Howells's experience of John Brown.

In the poems written directly on the topic of Brown, literosity continued supreme. They were not, of course, typically Heinesque. "Gerrit Smith" and "Old Brown" were, however, quite literose, trending to the common sin of "the false sublime." Brown was "an idea" to the poet, not a person, not a tragedy, not an occasion for war. Howells, as Gibson and Arms pointed out, dated "Old Brown" 26 November 1859. It appeared in the *Sentinel* for 25 January 1860. The hiatus suggests that it had gone to Lowell and been declined for the *Atlantic* before the *Sentinel* got it. It was instantly successful as an "exchange" item — what is more predictable in a newspaper than the advent of the false sublime? Thence James Redpath picked it up to anthologize in *Echoes of Harper's Ferry*.

Literary taste was no object of Redpath's. War was his game. But his treatment of "Old Brown" suggests that he had qualms about it even though he soon would seek refuge from the Mason Committee in Ashtabula County. *Echoes of Harper's Ferry* places "Old Brown" in "Book Fourth, Non-Resistants." There it is grouped with Whittier's "Brown of Ossawattomie"; an epistolary debate between Whittier and Garrison about whether Whittier was not too pacifistic; and a sermon by James Freeman Clarke. It was distinguished company, but Redpath thought it not sufficiently bellicose, not at the fighting core. Neither, of course, was father Howells or Giddings, Lincoln, or Salmon P. Chase. The break-through toward reality—surrounded by melodrama and propaganda, of course—came with "The Pilot's Story." It is still a remarkable poem. It not only thoroughly pleased the *Atlantic* set—hence Ticknor's pleasant little game of paying the price for it out to Howells in gold coin—it helped set the *Atlantic* position on the eve of Lincoln's election.

II

ODDLY WOVEN INTO THE EDGES of young Howells's life-stage as a provincial poet was the strange career of Salmon P. Chase. The *Ohio State Journal* was published by Henry Cooke in Howells's time. It supported the cause of Chase, who had a first-rate chance of becoming the Republican nominee but muffed it by being too high and mighty to solicit support and win the pledged unit support of a solid Ohio Republican delegation to the Chicago convention. Without that "favorite son" support, he faced a split Ohio delegation. The shock disconcerted his supporters from other states, and the door opened to Abraham Lincoln of Illinois.

Chase was able, cultivated, magnetic, and courageously antislavery.[1] He had contributed money to John Brown. Coming out of the Democratic party, he offered something different from old Whigs like Wade or Giddings—or even Lincoln. What Chase conspicuously lacked was what Giddings and Lincoln had in abundance—the common touch. Chase was a "white pine Yankee," a scholar and a gentleman. But he also was possessed by entirely too much of Charles Sumner's besetting sin: Yankee cultural and moral pride beyond the point of arrogance. When he might really have won the Republican nomination, he would not stoop to the mere politics of organizing and pledging the Republican delegation to a unit voice for him. Chaos followed.

As governor of Ohio with a table presided over by his brilliant, fated daughter Kate, Chase became personally important to Howells: the governor and his dazzling daughter took the lead in Columbus by fitting Howells for the great world by teaching him upper-class manners and dress. They prepped him for Boston. Meanwhile, Howells promoted the Chase cause in his work for the *Ohio State Journal*. Chase was politically easier for Howells to take than the Redpaths of the world. Like father Howells, Chase believed, as a Radical Republican should, in the extirpation of slavery, but he thought all violent solutions self-defeating. He wanted to hem in the South with Free States and let slavery wither on the vine. It was John Brown's terrorist inspiration that if he struck at Harpers Ferry and suffered Virginia to hang him for it, in no distant future he would raise up an Edmund Ruffin to fire on a Fort Sumter, and the peace option would be doomed.

Whether Chase's blunder into political suicide could be read in the cards by his backers or not, the *Ohio State Journal* found its cash flow practically dry in the early spring of 1860. Cooke had to fire most of his staff—and owe them back salary to boot. Howells compensated by hitting a streak of luck. The publishers of *Poems of Two Friends*, young, energetic, Republican, admired Howells and thought they could use his talents. Almost as soon as Lincoln won the nomination on 18 May, Follett and Foster assigned Howells to write a campaign biography of the Rail-splitter.

They had good reasons. The "West" needed a west-

erner's portrait of the Republican nominee. They liked
Howells's writing, wit, and political savvy. They needed
a quick, neat, brief introduction to an anthology of
speeches and other papers by Lincoln and his running
mate. They told Howells to finish in June and begin by
going to Springfield to interview Old Abe, get the facts,
and get cracking.

Perhaps the one odd feature in Howells's response was
that he did not go to Springfield. He commissioned somebody else to get his material. His later explanation, that
he missed "the chance of a life-time," as he said, because
he was too busy with a book of poems, strikes one as a
partial truth. He *was* busy with editing *The Poets and
Poetry of the West: with Biographical and Critical Notices*,
by William T. Coggeshall, a tome Follett and Foster
would publish at the end of the summer. But in his not
going to Springfield as in his not speaking to Lincoln to
thank him for his consular appointment, there lurks the
hint of suspicion that the young Howells misjudged Lincoln. Perhaps loyalty to Chase set Howells wrong. And
there was a political difference. The most radical Republicans were all-out warriors of the John Brown mold; but
most of the Radical Republicans would rather have let
the South secede and take slavery with it than fight to
keep them in. Lincoln, of course, was a Unionist. Not
until the signing of the Emancipation Proclamation
would the great bulk of Radical Republicans support the
Union war effort. As for everybody, history had its lessons for Howells.

No sense of resistance or conflict with Lincoln reveals
itself in Howells's little *Life*, however; he was too purely a
professional for that. In a week of hard work, he wrote an
often elegant, perceptive introduction: "spirited, flow-
ing, and graceful," said the Cincinnati *Commercial*. He
did understand Lincoln's frontier experience. One of

nine campaign biographies of Lincoln, Howells's picked
up a unique importance to Lincoln biographers because
Lincoln twice withdrew it from the Library of Congress,
and he so annotated it in pencil for a friend that it has
been argued that what he did not correct is accurate, and
so Howells's little book became an authoritative source
for Lincoln biography.[2]

The good little book had good reviews and made a
little very important money. And it was an act, a deed of
real politics in the real, masculine American world. Care-
fully middle-keeping, never suggesting anything that
would be used against Lincoln, the book showed that
Howells could use the poet and journalist in him to
support the politician. Therefore the book says nothing
of John Brown. But his influence was there, urging Howells to combative action, to strike a blow. It would all
unite at last to effects that changed the course and devel-
opment of Howells's life.

III

COLUMBUS AND EVEN OHIO had begun to out-
live their usefulness to Howells. He began to yearn to get
out of the provinces as once he had longed and fought to
get out of the small town. Why did he not, said Follett and
Foster, take the early royalties on the Lincoln book and
invest the money in a trip East? There he could investigate the new industries about which the West was cur-
ious. He could write "travel letters" to Ohio papers and
no doubt collect them into a book after he got home.
Howells's heart leaped – not at the mills and plants about
which he hardly could have cared less. His heart leaped
at the freedom to go East – to Boston and the *Atlantic*
and the great writers; to New York and the *Saturday Press*
and literary Gotham. Maybe he could get a job there!

He launched the pilgrimage that was to become famous in American literary history, however, with a strange act of literary and political defiance blended. He was to write two series of travel letters, one for the *Ohio State Journal* and the other for the Cincinnati *Gazette*. But the one entitled "Letters from the Country" is unique, a series of one item, dated 30 June 1860 and published (by design?) in the Fourth of July number of the *Ohio State Journal*, where it appears beside the ritual reprinting of the Declaration of Independence.

Howells's "Country" letter is really a sketch, ostensibly reporting on his journey by rail and stage from Columbus to his home village of "Anyplace, Nowhere, Ohio." The tone is that of Irving in his excursions into romantic irony and mockery. But it has a fine snapper on the end for anyone who kept John Brown's men in mind. There is persiflage about the agonies of getting up to catch a train leaving at four A.M. On the stagecoach, grotesques, mostly female and reminiscent of Irving and Dickens, practice almost insane eccentricities. But our attention is increasingly drawn to a sleepy sunbrowned youth, obviously worn with fatigue:

> He looked old and young, and there was a sadness in his face, of which, however, the lines were sharply and decisively cut. A virgin sweetness—that seemed, somehow, to be a remembered trait—hovered about his mouth. . . .

When the stage reaches the end of the line and the writer is at home, he learns "that the unknown young man was Barclay Coppoc, one of John Brown's men."

A number of issues seem to run together in "Letter from the Country." Howells was almost surely in Jefferson on 30 June. In one sense his firecracker saluted Marshal Freyer, in another it bragged in Columbus of the security of John Brown's men in Ashtabula. Coppoc was worn with far travel (from Springdale?) and, no doubt, anxiety—he was still one of the most wanted men in the country. In Anywhere, Nowhere, Ashtabula, he could sleep like a child, perfectly secure in the public stage. Anyone who knows the faces of men not long from combat will recognize the physiognomy Howells saw in the slumbering Coppoc. And yet there is also something in the sketch reminiscent of the Andover Band's shivaree for John Brown, Jr., at Dorset. Howells wanted to shock, to sound a mocking defiance from Ashtabula County to the world. Nevertheless, there is an undertone of "Goodbye to all that" in his "Letter." He was moving on—he hoped.

IV

HIS FIRST REGULAR TRAVEL LETTER, "Glimpses of Summer Travel" for the *Gazette*, was dated "Buffalo"; and he was on his way to Niagara Falls. He was taking the most picturesque and "foreign" route, the one best calculated to provide copy. He had also stepped into something like a mythical dream of youth's argosy. As in a mythical journey, one voyage would lead to another, adventures stretching far away, and many a struggle until he triumphed. He would even go back to Columbus for one more and the best of his years there; but the argosy began when he caught that four A.M. train for Cleveland in June 1860.

Before that, however, he had written a poem, perhaps the best of his early poetic period, that would win him a hearty welcome when he got to Boston. At the time when Follett and Foster wanted him to go to Springfield and see Lincoln, it is possible that the poetic project that held him in Columbus was not to polish off Coggeshall's anthology but to put a high finish on "The Pilot's Story."

Almost nobody knows it, no casual reader would find it; I think it is better to present the poem itself than to "explicate" it without a text. It does show to what the John Brown impulse released Howells. It would appear in the September 1860 *Atlantic*.

THE PILOT'S STORY

I.

It was a story the pilot told, with his back to his hearers. —
Keeping his hand on the wheel and his eye on the globe of the
    jack-staff,
Holding the boat to the shore and out of the sweep of the
    current,
Lightly turning aside for the heavy logs of drift-wood,
Widely shunning the snags that made us sardonic obeisance.

II.

All the soft, damp air was full of delicate perfume
From the young willows in bloom on either bank of the
    river, —
Faint, delicious fragrance, trancing the indolent senses
In a luxurious dream of the river and land of the lotus. ·
Not yet out of the west the roses of sunset were withered;
In the deep blue above light clouds of gold and of crimson
Floated in slumber serene, and the restless river beneath
    them
Rushed away to the sea with a vision of rest in its bosom.
Far on the eastern shore lay dimly the swamps of the
    cypress;
Dimly before us the islands grew from the river's expanses, —
Beautiful, wood-grown isles, — with the gleam of the swart
    inundation
Seen through the swaying boughs and slender trunks of their
    willows;
And on the shore beside us the cotton-trees rose in the
    evening,
Phantom-like, yearningly, wearily, with the inscrutable
    sadness
Of the mute races of trees. While hoarsely the steam from
    her 'scape-pipes

Shouted, then whispered a moment, then shouted again to
   the silence,
Trembling through all her frame with the mighty pulse of
   her engines,
Slowly the boat ascended the swollen and broad Mississippi,
Bank-full, sweeping on, with nearing masses of drift-wood,
Daintily breathed about with hazes of silvery vapor,
Where in his arrowy flight the twittering swallow alighted,
And the belated blackbird paused on the way to its
   nestlings.

   III.

It was the pilot's story: — "They both came aboard there,
   at Cairo,
From a New Orleans boat, and took passage with us for
   Saint Louis.
She was a beautiful woman, with just enough blood from
   her mother,
Darkening her eyes and her hair, to make her race known
   to a trader:
You would have thought she was white. The man that was
   with her, — you see such,
Weakly good-natured and kind, and weakly good-natured and
   vicious,
Slender of body and soul, fit neither for loving nor hating.
I was a youngster then, and only learning the river, —
Not over-fond of the wheel. I used to watch them at *monte*,
Down in the cabin at night, and learned to know all of
   the gamblers.
So when I saw this weak one staking his money
   against them,
Betting upon the turn of the cards, I knew what was coming:
They never left their pigeons a single feather to fly with.
Next day I saw them together, — the stranger and one of the
   gamblers:
Picturesque rascal he was, with long black hair and
   moustaches,
Black slough hat drawn down to his eyes from his villainous
   forehead:
On together they moved, still earnestly talking in whispers
On toward the forecastle, where sat the woman alone by the
   gangway

Roused by the fall of feet, she turned, and, beholding her
    master,
Greeted him with a smile that was more like a wife's than
    another's,
Rose to meet him fondly, and then, with the dread
    apprehension
Always haunting the slave, fell her eye on the face of the
    gambler,
Dark and lustful and fierce and full of merciless cunning.
Something was spoken so low that I could not hear what the
    words were;
Only the woman started, and looked from one to the other,
With imploring eyes, bewildered hands, and a tremor
All through her frame: I saw her from where I was standing,
    she shook so.
'Say! it is so?' she cried. On the weak, white lips of
    her master
Died a sickly smile, and he said, — 'Louise, I have sold you.'
God is my judge! May I never see such a look of despairing,
Desolute anguish, as that which the woman cast on her
    master,
Gripping her breast with her little hands, as if he had
    stabbed her,
Standing in silence a space, as fixed as the Indian woman,
Carved out of wood, on the pilot-house of the old Pocahontas!
Then, with a gurgling moan, like the sound in the throat
    of the dying,
Came back her voice, that, rising, fluttered, through
    wild incoherence,
Into a terrible shriek that stopped my heart while she
    answered: —
Sold me? sold me? sold — And you promised to give me
    my freedom! —
Promised me, for the sake of our little boy in Saint Louis!
What will you say to our boy, when he cries for me there
    in Saint Louis?
What will you say to our God? — Ah, you have been joking!
    I see it! —
No? God! God! He shall hear it, — And all of the angels
    in heaven, —
Even the devils in hell! — and none will believe when they
    hear it!

Sold me!'—Fell her voice with a thrilling wail, and in
  silence
Down she sank on the deck, and covered her face with her
  fingers."

  IV.

In his story a moment the pilot paused, while we listened
To the salute of a boat, that, rounding the point of an
  island,
Flamed toward us with fires that seemed to burn from the
  waters,—
Stately and vast and swift, and borne on the heart of
  the current.
Then, with the mighty voice of a giant challenged to
  battle,
Rose the responsive whistle, and all the echoes of
  island,
Swamp-land, glade, and brake replied with a myriad clamor,
Like wild birds that are suddenly startled from slumber
  at midnight;
Then were at peace once more, and we heard the harsh cries
  of the peacocks
Perched on a tree by a cabin-door, where the white-headed
  settler's
White-headed children stood to look at the boat as it
  passed them,
Passed them so near that we heard their happy talk and
  their laughter.
Softly the sunset had faded, and now on the eastern
  horizon
Hung, like a tear in the sky, the beautiful star of the
  evening.

  V.

Still with his back to us standing, the pilot went on
  with his story:—
"Instantly, all the people, with looks of reproach and
  compassion,
Flocked around the prostrate woman. The children cried,
  and their mothers
Hugged them tight to their breasts; but the gambler said
  to the captain,—

'Put me off there at the town that lies round the bend
    of the river.
Here, you! rise at once, and be ready now to go with me.'
Roughly he seized the woman's arm and strove to uplift her.
She—she seemed not to heed him, but rose like one that
    is dreaming,
Slid from his grasp, and fleetly mounted the steps of the
    gangway,
Up to the hurricane-deck, in silence, without lamentation.
Straight to the stern of the boat, where the wheel was,
    she ran, and the people
Followed her fast till she turned and stood at bay for a
    moment,
Looking them in the face, and in the face of the gambler.
Not one to save her,—not one of all the compassionate
    people!
Not one to save her, of all the pitying angels in heaven!
Not one bolt of God to strike him dead there before her!
Wildly she waved him back, we waiting in silence and horror.
Over the swarthy face of the gambler a pallor of passion
Passed like a gleam of lightning over the west in the
    night-time.
White, she stood, and mute, till he put forth his hand to
    secure her;
Then she turned and leaped,—in mid air fluttered a moment,—
Down, there, whirling, fell, like a broken-winged bird
    from a tree-top,
Down on the cruel wheel, that caught her, and hurled her,
    and crushed her,
And in the foaming water plunged her, and hid her forever."

    VI.

Still with his back to us all the pilot stood, but we
    heard him
Swallowing hard, as he pulled the bell-rope to stop her.
Then, turning,—
"This is the place where it happened," brokenly whispered
    the pilot.
"Somehow, I never like to go by here alone in the night-
    time."
Darkly the Mississippi flowed by the town that lay in the
    starlight,

Cheerful with lamps. Below we could hear them reversing
 the engines,
And the great boat glided up to the shore like a giant
 exhausted.
Heavily sighed her pipes. Broad over the swamps to the
 eastward
Shone the full moon, and turned our far-trembling wake
 into silver.
All was serene and calm, but the odorous breath of the
 willows
Smote like the subtile breath of an infinite sorrow
 upon us.

The poem was altogether American; nothing in it existed or could have happened in England. One could say
a number of literary things about its art, but this is not the
right context. Howells later thought there was a good deal
of realism in it. The steamboat lore would be the best in
American literature until Howells coaxed "Old Times on
the Mississippi" out of Clemens. And it was aggressive,
hard-hitting propaganda in total effect. It struck a blow
for the right as Howells saw the right. And he had taken
the eyes of his imagination off his artificial poetic self to
focus them on a national political and moral dilemma. As
he would tell young Stephen Crane thirty-five years after,
what counts is "perspective."

Howells sent "The Pilot's Story" ahead of himself to the
Atlantic, where they not only accepted it with approbation but Ticknor himself paid him on the spot and in
gold, laying down the coins one by one and ceremoni-
ously by way of honor.

I think there is no parallel for the cordiality extended to
Howells by the *Atlantic* set in Boston. Though he did not
see "literary Boston," he did see the authors of most of the
best literature then being produced in New England and,
as a matter of course, generally published in the *Atlantic*.
The prime mover in the event was Lowell, and among

Lowell's many motives there was a political component. Lowell was well aware what debts the Republican party in Massachusetts owed to Ohio in general and Joshua R. Giddings in particular. In Lowell's radical youth, he had been a Giddings fan, going so far as to write a sonnet that he used to close and climax his first volume of *Poems*, 1844.

TO J. R. GIDDINGS

Giddings, far rougher names than thine have grown
Smoother than honey on the lips of men;
And thou shalt aye be honorably known,
As one who bravely used his tongue and pen,
As best befits a freeman,—even for those
To whom our Law's unblushing front denies
A right to plead against the lifelong woes
Which are the Negro's glimpse of Freedom's skies:
Fear nothing, and hope all things, as the Right
Alone may do securely; every hour
The thrones of Ignorance and ancient Night
Lose somewhat of their long-usurpëd power,
And Freedom's lightest word can make them shiver
With a base dread that clings to them forever.[3]

Howells remembered that, "in all the talk," nothing political was discussed, despite the date, by or among Lowell, Holmes, and Fields. It would have been impossible. They knew among themselves where they had agreed to agree and disagree. They could well suspect that, in one way or another, they would disagree with Howells about John Brown. Courtesy restrained them. Nevertheless, Howells profited by their sense of a debt to Ohio and Giddings—and to their representative. Howells found no such welcome at the *Saturday Press* or from the Bohemian set. It was back into egotism.

Lowell, no longer the ardent reformer he had been with Maria White, his first wife, had still returned vigorously into American reform politics when he took up the *Atlan-*

tic. He was not dealing in radical imperatives any more, but he was serious and militant about his antislavery stance, attacking slashingly as occasion offered. He accepted articles by T. W. Higginson and Theodore Parker,[4] and they were two members of John Brown's "Secret Six" money-raising team. Lowell had good reason for a measure of political gratitude. And Fields and Ticknor published Lowell's *Atlantic*, and Holmes was Lowell's friend.

Simply, then, to read the gorgeous welcome Howells found among the *Atlantic* set as a purely literary affair is naïve. Nobody in it was a "John Brown man," nobody openly agreed with Emerson or Thoreau or Wendell Phillips. They knew that among John Brown men Howells was suspect as a temporizing nonresistant, a peace man, and at that point they agreed with him. They liked what they read in "The Pilot's Story": to publish it in September 1860 helped place the magazine behind Lincoln for the imminent elections. They had no job for Howells, nothing but cordiality, applause, and good advice. But what they gave would help a young man from the provinces for two decades to come. Above all else, just now, they stiffened his faith to believe that he could escape from the provinces and live significantly in the great world.

V

PROFESSIONALLY, when neither Boston nor New York would yield a job, Howells came back to Columbus, where he still had a job, and was met by a delightful surprise. Presumably in support of Lincoln's campaign, Henry Cooke was in funds again. He revived the fainting *Ohio State Journal*, paid Howells his back pay, and rehired him. It was to be the last and best of Howells's Columbus years, and he would launch two of his life's most fateful argosies before 1861 was out: marriage and expatriation.

He went on writing for the *Atlantic* and the *Saturday Press*. Significantly, he did "correspondence" from Ohio to the New York *World*. The story of his courtship and engagement, fateful to him though it was to be, is almost without connection to the present context. To be sure, Elinor Mead came from a good Republican family, and one of the reasons she had come to Ohio was to see her kinsman Rutherford B. Hayes, already a power in the Republican party in Cincinnati. Except that Howells's politics counted for and not against him as a suitor, then, they mattered little to the greatest adventure of his 1861: meeting, courting, and somehow becoming quietly engaged to Elinor. When he could be married, however, depended obviously on the yet unsolved question of a career. The immediate solution turned out to be a consular appointment to Venice, and that became a matter of the plainest, most practical politics. The solution became all the more urgent when Cooke, again short of funds, sold out and left for Washington, again owing Howells some of his pay.

The answer Howells sought by following him. He wrote Chase to solicit his good offices. Father Howells sent a plea to Senator Wade, probably drawn up by James A. Garfield, and signed by a number of Ohio worthies. Apparently Chase spoke to Lincoln and Wade forwarded his document, probably adding a note of his own. Lincoln then apparently turned the matter over to John G. Nicolay, who was with John Hay one of Lincoln's brilliant team of private secretaries. Both aspired to forward the cause of "Western poetry," knew Howells's work, and admired him. Nobody knowing just which the post would be, Howells thus "made the list" of "deserving Republicans" to whom some place, some feasible consulate would be awarded. After much hauling and tugging, and without

Howells's having in the least intended it, he became U.S. consul at Venice, one of the best places on earth for him at that moment. It did not matter that Howells had no idea how good Venice was but took it because the salary, raised for wartime reasons, was enough to get married on.

"To the victor belong the spoils." So runs that law of combat which Andrew Jackson fixed in our political process so firmly that it rules still. In Lincoln's day there were no civil service laws, no bureaucratic empires built strong enough to defy presidents. Everything was up for grabs, and the pressures of office-seeking drove Lincoln almost to distraction. Add to that the impending war, and life in Washington raged almost out of control. Even Howells with all his contacts and prospects was close to dismay. As he wrote his father, "Washington is a most heart-sickening place—the Disappointed throng the streets like uneasy ghost, and refuse to believe themselves hopeless."[5] One of those uneasy ghosts, who went home hopeless, was Herman Melville. Nobody knew him; he was not among the "deserving."

What made Howells so? His father's record of lifelong devotion to the antislavery cause and his sufferings in it. His newspaper leadership of Free-Soil and Republican pioneering with Giddings and the Western Reserve. Howells's record in Columbus and his favor with Chase. The campaign biography. And the support not only of giants like Chase and Wade but of representative Ohio Republicans without dissent. All these credentials he had and the practical political know-how (backed by his father's wisdom) to use them.

Finally, he was a poet. That he was a "Western" poet was all to the good in the dawn of the Ohio period. Had Hay or Nicolay known Herman Melville—as Van Buren, for instance, might have known him or at least have been accessible—Melville's merely literary desert would have

carried him far. One of the few redeeming traditions of
the spoils system had been the happy inspiration that
often sent American authors abroad to occupy foreign
service posts. Irving in Spain was the classic example.
Howells stood out among the ranks of Republican victors.
Somebody was going to get the spoils: why not he, poet,
politician, even the propaganda poet of "The Pilot's
Story"?

Fifty-one years later, speaking at the great dinner held
for Howells's seventy-fifth birthday, President William
Howard Taft would point with pride to Howells's career as
a justification of the presidential appointment system.
Looking back autobiographically, Howells would see that
the Venetian appointment "was the beginning of the best
luck I have had in the world. . . ."[6]

As of the present in 1861, he felt only that it was something he must do; everybody said so. Thereby the politician, even the radical, in Howells served the poet.

CHAPTER FIVE
FROM EMPIRE TO ERIECREEK

O NCE AT VENICE, Howells found in effect everything to do. With time he became sophisticated in the language and much of the literature. He learned Venetian painting, architecture, and history. More important, he studied the common people in their streets and plazas, learning that trick of cross-cultural insight to which he would later subject American life. But perhaps his greatest gain was a new political sophistication. By watching sympathetically the struggles of a resisting people against an imperial occupation of their ancient city, he learned what liberty and democracy mean as he had never understood them before — from the underside, from the point of view of deprivation.

I

VENICE IN HOWELLS'S TIME was feebly and foolishly occupied by the decaying Hapsburg Empire, itself the relict of the Holy Roman Empire. A second, confusedly related, equally decadent secular empire lay nearby in the then Papal States. And of course Venice itself was the beautiful shell of a great maritime empire from which the positive vital life had long ago shriveled away into death. "I lived in Italy in the Garibaldi days, when he was still a god, and the gondoliers expected him as in a second coming," Howells told Sir George Otto Trevelyan.[1]

By good luck or happy advice, Howells discovered at once in Venice that the Venetians were committed to

intense campaigns of passive resistance against the Austrians. If you wished to know Venetians, you must ignore
Austrians and their followers. All Howells's democratic
training and Radical Republican sympathy joined to
place him in solidarity with the Venetians. And they
yearned passionately to be reached and saved (as indeed
they shortly would be) in the *Risorgimento*, Garibaldi's
newness, the Kingdom of Italy. So strong were their
passions that comic scenes occasionally resulted. Moncure D. Conway remembered in his *Autobiography* that,
when he was Howells's guest in Venice, "one day a beautiful Italian countess breakfasted with us. She . . . talked
eloquently about the wrongs of Venice. She lit a large
cigar, but even that did not console her; her tears flowed
down on the cigar . . . " (429).

No matter how extravagant, however, the Venetian
passion for self-determination was real. Howells's sympathy, equally sincere, opened Venetian hearts and
doors. In turn Howells's eyes were opened to the real
Venice, and *Venetian Life* became possible — "the book
that made friends with fortune for me," as he once called
it.[2] More significantly, he found confirming itself before
his eyes the American faith that ancient Europe meant
tyranny and decadence. His applications of that perception to the American scene were to inform his mature
work.

Venice trained Howells's eye also to see the truth
about the end-games of empire. Venice dead and Aus-
tria decadent were at once shoddy, cruel, and mean-
ingless. And the trope most sharply yet subtly etched to
register just those impressions in *Venetian Life* related the
pilgrimage Howells tried to make to the monastery of a
seventeenth-century hero of the Venetian Republic,
Paolo Sarpi. According to Howells, Sarpi was a pure and
faithful brother of the Servite order who had the patri-

otism and genius to rescue Venice from an unjust papal interdict.

Sarpi had the energy, statesmanship, integrity, courage, and polemical skill sufficient to defy the interdict, defend the city, and at length compel the pope to recall his bull. Part of Sarpi's power was the will to survive multiple stab wounds after papal assassins had ambushed him. He was a true hero of anti-imperialism in an age of empire, and Venice had forgotten him.

It was restoring the ruins of his monastery for use as an asylum for "indigent and abandoned women" to be cared for by an order of nuns. Nobody remembered Sarpi. His grave had been dug up, the stone shattered. On the grass outside the walls, a squad of Hungarian soldiers from an Austrian regiment engaged loudly in bayonet practice—noisily intruding the presence of the Occupation. Inside the walls, where they knew no Sarpi, were broken statuary, an excavation, "—and everywhere also the unnameable filth with which ruin is always dishonored in Italy, and which makes the most picturesque and historic places inaccessible to the foot, and intolerable to the senses and the soul" (210).

Surrounded by human turds stood a heap of the exhumed bones of old Servites. "The friars' skulls looked contented enough," remarked the narrator, "and smiled after the hearty manner of skulls; and some of the legbones were thrust through the enclosing fence, and hung rakishly over the top" (211). In net conclusion, the tale turns, then, as ironic and reductive of holy empire as anything in Mark Twain's *The Innocents Abroad*, which had not yet become a gleam in Clemens's preconscious vision:

> So far as the life-long presence and the death of a man of clear brain and true heart could hallow any scene, this ground was holy; for here Sarpi lived, and here in his cell he

died, a simple Servite friar—he who had caught the bolts of excommunication launched against the Republic from Rome, and broken them in his hand,—who had breathed upon the mighty arm of the temporal power, and withered it to the juiceless stock it now remains. And yet I could not feel that the ground *was* holy, and it did not make me think of Sarpi, and I believe that only those travellers who invent in cold blood their impressions of memorable places ever have impressions to record. (212)

The first great triumph of the American Republic had been to set at nought the ancient law of revolutions: they begin in war upon an intolerable tyranny, pass to the unstable success of an ill-designed republic, disintegrate into a chaos of pure democracy that demands the control of a man on a white horse, and he, at last, restores tyranny. Washington's sort of republican virtue, aided by the character and genius of the other Founding Fathers, saved the United States, it was believed. Countless treatises were written, and in many countries, contrasting the outcomes of the American and the French revolutions. The fathers had given us "the world's fairest hope," but left it fatally "linked with man's foulest crime."

There stood another image, feared by Jefferson and John Adams, versified by Philip Freneau and William Cullen Bryant, of the destruction of republican simplicity through arrogance, extravagance, and irresponsibility. Thomas Cole painted it, unforgettably to the Americans of his time, in a set of panels called *The Course of Empire*. Primitive wilderness progressed to republican virtue, simplicity, and happiness. Perverted into power and grandeur, into pride and domination, empire rose upon the ashes of virtue. But empire turned to decadence and impotency, opening the gates to the barbarian with fire and rapine. At last the broken wall and column half-covered with encroaching wilderness beside the empty harbor united to show the cycle's end—the return to dust.

Howells might well have held such images in mind when he studied the end-games of empire in Venice. *Venetian Life* at one point or another suggests that its author kept such themes in mind. Certainly no later than the middle 1850s, the Free-Soil and new Republican polemicists were adapting the Washingtonian and imperial myths for their own purpose. The *Ashtabula Sentinel* and young Howells in his *Ohio State Journal* column habitually mocked exponents of the proslavery argument as "the chivalry." They anticipated Mark Twain's charge that the Civil War was the child of "Sir Walter Scottism" in the South. And they anticipated the Unionist contention that the war had to be fought and won to debar decadence, sin, and imperialism, all southern, from destroying the Republic.

The most attractive of Unionist themes, it justified Unionist and Radical Republican to one another, catching up even Emerson together with Melville. To argue that slavery was decadent, a vestigial remnant of feudalism imported from bloody Europe, justified Lincoln in saying that in Union victory lay "the last, best hope of earth." The irony of slavery's historical connection to American democracy led Melville in his poem "Misgivings (1860)" to report:

> I muse upon my country's ills—
> The tempest bursting from the waste of Time
> On the world's fairest hope linked with man's
> foulest crime.

So regarded, the wartime sacrifice seemed to have been offered up and the victory won for modernity, righteousness, the democratic dream, and the national destiny. To find, on the wings of postwar northern euphoria, the

Howellsian irony scouring away at the squalors of Europe gratified even the Unionist in grief for his losses.

After the Emancipation Proclamation, Howells like other Radical Republicans could join the Union cause. No doubt several of his many rather distinguished American visitors, touring Europe without concern for the war, helped him grasp the fullness of the Union justification, and he would work it subtly into his book. Now he could feel reconciled to a crusade against "man's foulest crime." Now he could see his friends the young generals — Hayes and Garfield, Mitchell and Comly — as moral heroes. To stalwarts of the Union propaganda effort like Norton and Godkin and Lowell, a well-accredited, "lifelong" antislavery man turned Union idealist also seemed just right. They gave him enthusiastic support.

II

NOT UNLIKE THE RETURNING SOLDIERS, Howells came home from Venice with his career all to make. Venice had done its office for him; he could not stay and stagnate with the lagoons. He aimed for the highest he knew — a successful literary career — but he knew he must start the climb up his mountain from "a basis." That meant a salaried job for security while he wrote his way to the status of established author.

He turned his back on chances in Ohio, even friendly offers to buy him a city newspaper to edit. Two roads diverged, and he chose not to go the way of Whitelaw Reid, for instance. Instead, he tried New York again, not unfairly offering himself as an experienced political reporter. They would take him on as a free-lance or "stringer," but they offered him no basis. The record of what he placed in the New York *Times*, the Cincinnati *Gazette*, and the *Nation* until his basis came speaks for his sophistication and force as a political reporter, among other things. Finally, on 17 November 1865, he concluded negotiations with E. L. Godkin, the great editor of the freshest, most rewarding periodical in New York, the *Nation*. For a "basis" of forty dollars a week plus freedom to market elsewhere as he could, Howells went to work for Godkin.

Some of his topics provide excellent windows into the qualities of a mind, once radically trained, in the midst of the true American Gilded Age. Postwar, that mind remained profoundly critical of what developed from the age—which was just what Godkin wanted. Godkin, like his New England backers, was deadly serious. They had set themselves (probably not quite knowing it) against what appears to be something like a real rule of history: to win a major war, one must convert the common civilian morality into combat morality. Combat morality obeys the rule of kill or be killed. It also decrees that, to achieve victory, everything and everybody is expendable.

The rules of military morality regarding life and property are the crimes of civilian morality. If no new war intervenes, it may take a generation to establish a new civilian morality, and virtue will be severely afflicted in the meanwhile. Godkin, with Norton and his other wealthy backers of the *Nation*, believed the Unionist dream. They believed what Henry James said he all innocently believed until the unthinkable catastrophe of the suicide of Europe in World War I: "Just after the Civil War," Americans like him felt "publicly purged of the dreadful disease which had come within an inch of being fatal to us, and . . . warranted sound forever, superlatively safe."

The *Nation* intended first and always to exert every influence to hold the country up to the ideal virtue bought with blood and agony. Many a major American mind thought it could be done, and Howells, still young, agreed. Through the gathering disappointments of the 1860s and for six more decades to come, he would never cease to fight, after his style, to redeem the promise. He got the *Nation*'s job because he believed and wrote effectively in support of the promise. But he also got it because western humor and Heine and a now well-practiced irony armed him to fight with one of the best of American political weapons—laughter. Godkin knew he could not win with nothing but heavy moral blasting. He needed variety and the public appeal of ridicule in that palmiest age of American humor. He had been looking for his man for months until he concluded that Howells was the one he wanted.

His new man delivered, too. Primarily he wrote a weekly column entitled "Minor Topics." In mode it was not unlike Howells's "News and Humors of the Mail" from Columbus, but it rose to a first-class New York level. Godkin was delighted. Though he was austere, he became Howells's friend for life. Besides the deft touches of wit and irony, Howells did not hesitate to enter upon major considerations. He had his say on democracy: more to be prized than European "history, art, and the poetry of association" is "that social and civil life which permits every life to be at once grand and simple, that makes man superior to classes and only subject to free-.dom." What more could father Howells or Walt Whitman or, indeed, John Brown ask for? Again, he argued "that in democratic theory all labor is, and in democratic practice all labor should be, equally honorable. . . . " He defended the Negro against pseudo-scientific canards.

All of the foregoing Howells might have written in Columbus or even Jefferson, Ohio. Venice, however, had above all else trained him to look about him and see plainly; it had given him a true use of his eyes. What he saw in New York and from the elevated perspective of the *Nation* was the Gilded Age in the first flush of its postwar application of military morality to the *res publica* and the people as victims. His reactions were angry.

He lambasted venal politicians and callous robber barons, especially in their conduct of the new railroad industry. He registered the social horrors of New York, compounded by corruptly inept city government, and protested. One needed to look far to parallel New York: "while it rivals Naples in the filth of its streets," it "may well challenge the most favored regions of California to equal the daring and impunity of its brigands." He had "made it," with rich future promise, in New York. But almost exactly as soon as the fact was apparent, James T. Fields appeared and hired him away to the job Fields had denied him in 1860. On 1 March 1866, his twenty-ninth birthday, Howells began as assistant editor of the *Atlantic Monthly*, then by far the most influential magazine in the United States. The press all over the country reverberated to the shock of recognition that a westerner (and an old radical at that) had arrived. In a sense, Dr. Holmes's little joke about "apostolic succession" had turned from fancy into reality.

III

HIS *NATION* AND FREE-LANCE political pieces from New York join with Howells's relatively slight political writing as assistant editor on the *Atlantic* to suggest that he felt neither elated nor downcast by the onset of the Gilded Age. Like the Walt Whitman of *Democratic Vistas*, Howells knew too much about practical politics to allow himself to be plunged into despair: practical problems yield to practical solutions. He had never believed that freeing the slaves would open the gates to the Promised Land. Freedom was a national necessity; he did not expect an abatement of sin to achieve heaven on earth. It had never struck him either that a Union triumph would bring about utopia, not even a moral security, "superlatively safe." Therefore the events of Johnson's and Grant's incredible administrations did not shock the ironist. They did, however, in the presence of confusions altogether unforeseen, set him to groping for adequate responses. And the one response he clearly found at least minimally adequate he also called "radical": the preservation of fundamental democratic decencies.

In his own literary work as in his frequent reviewing, even in his correspondence with *Atlantic* authors, Howells during his six years as assistant editor grew rapidly toward the art of the novel and the realistic mode in fiction. Then and ever after, he identified realism with democracy. After the success of *Venetian Life* and *Italian Journeys*, it struck him that perhaps his Venetian method might work well in Cambridge: nobody had studied common American life with the same detached yet sympathetic eye. He experimented with sketches for the *Atlantic*, found them well-received, and did a volume of *Suburban Sketches*.

Howells was moving toward mastery of a double-edged irony. It cut one way against the vulgarity and levity of the common people who squandered their opportunities for a life of democratic self-respect and happiness. But it bit deep at the other edge into "aristocratic" pride and fatuity. For, after all, no American can be "an American aristocrat"—the very term is a metaphor whether it is used positively or pejoratively. Walt Whitman had moods very like both of Howells's. The insuperable difficulty between them was the transcendental faith always there to save Whitman's democratic vista. Agnostic Howells belonged to the next generation. They knew no transcendent epiphanies. They felt a certain respect for the great idealists, but they scorned "idealizers."

The next advance Howells made upon realism came in *Their Wedding Journey*, one of his most popular books, not yet a novel but a blend of vacation travel on the honeymoon route to Niagara Falls and back down the St. Lawrence River. There he felt ready to let his implied narrator indulge, like Thackeray, in "authorial asides." One of those has been quoted often by critics who seem never to register the tensions of its ironies: "Ah! poor Real Life, which I love, can I make others share the delight I find in thy foolish and insipid face?" But there are others, seldom or never quoted, which let one guess pretty nearly where Howells stood just then. For instance, the following might almost have appeared in "The Editor's Study" two decades later. The condition in which to "seek" the common man as a subject for art, he said, is "in his habitual moods of vacancy and tiresomeness. To me, at any rate, he is at such times very precious; and I never perceive him to be so much a man and a brother as when I feel the pressure of his vast, natural, unaffected dullness. Then I am able to enter confidently into his life and inhabit there" (86–87).

In the years just after the war, Howells remained a hesitant, gainsaying Republican; but he stuck with the party as long as he could because it seemed preferable to the practical alternatives. He reviewed, along with *belles lettres*, histories, including those of Motley and Parkman, a number of Civil War memoirs, and various other political or metapolitical volumes. Allowing for the *Atlantic* requirements of style, tone, and treatment, through it all he kept the radical faith, praising Lecky's feminism, Higginson's love for the black soldier, and democratic tendency wherever he could find it.

When he became *Atlantic* editor in 1871, he experimented with "departments," one of which was "Politics." But it did not succeed, even though Howells wrote a few essays himself. The one thing his *Atlantic* seemed able to do was to print pioneering muckrakers. Howells began as early as John A. Coleman's "The Fight of a Man with a Railroad" in 1872; by the end of the decade, he would be publishing Henry Demarest Lloyd himself. In literature one of his finest moves opened the *Atlantic* to southern writers both as a true gesture of reconciliation and a way of redeeming the magazine's promise to be national, not just of New England.

Yet, as matters turned out, what the no longer "young" but still "early" Howells accomplished metamorphosized his radical training. His fiction did not suppress his thought and convictions. It exploited them, demonstrating the depths at which his radical education informed his creative imagination. His fictional power waxed dominant from one book to the next, suppressing the journalist in him and largely usurping the powers of the poet until they broke free again in the 1890s. Most importantly, in his radical habits of mind the early novelist discovered thematics that would recur throughout his long career. Not surprisingly, at one of the most fateful of turning points, he found a vivid image of John Brown standing to point his way.

IV

THERE WAS A LONG CREATIVE FIGHT, with much revision, before the author of *A Chance Acquaintance* forced his preconscious perception, his *donnée*, out into the light of rational definition. After the novel was done and he knew it had succeeded, he explained its key both to Henry James and to father Howells. Made quite different by the broad differences between his two correspondents, those explanations rank among the most important Howells ever wrote by way of defining his fictional intent. Not only do they concern the first in his long line of published novels, they set down considerations that would, with many a variant, provide the *données* of most of his novels (most of them superior) to come.

To be editor, in the footsteps of Lowell and Fields, of the *Atlantic* when it spoke with an authority respected from Boston to San Francisco placed Howells on ambition's highest peak. If Dr. Holmes recalled his little joke, one wonders what he thought. We can be sure Howells had not forgotten. He was only thirty-four and had not quite launched upon a novelist's career even with the great success of *Their Wedding Journey*. He would mature into higher ambitions. Still, as of the moment the question stood, naturally, "What next?" *A Chance Acquaintance* was the answer. As he wrestled with his art and his imagination for a clear sight of its "given," he learned that he had definitively crossed the line from travel-writer to novelist and that he had achieved central insights into the sort of novelist he could become.

Henry James admired *A Chance Acquaintaince* (it introduced "The American Girl" to the literary age) and wrote Howells to say so. Howells responded in a letter of thanks that probably echoes some of the long conversations about the nature of the novel in which James and Howells had spent hours, out walking or sitting together in Howells's study:

> First let me thank you with all my heart for your criticism on my story—rather, on my heroine. It came too late for the magazine; but I have been able to check the young person a

little before handing her down to the latest posterity in book form. Her pertness was but another proof of the contrariness of her sex: I meant her to be everything that was lovely, and went on protesting that she was so, but she preferred being saucy to the young man, especially in that second number. Afterwards I think she is at least all I profess for her. I like her because she seems to me a character: the man, I own is a simulacrum. Well or ill advisedly I conceived the notion of confronting two extreme American types; the conventional and the unconventional. These always disgust each other, but I amused myself with the notion of their falling in love, which would not be impossible, if they were both young and good looking. Now conventionality is, in our condition of things, in itself a caricature; I did my best for the young man, but his nature was against him, and he is the stick you see. Of course the girl must be attracted by what is elegant and fine in him, and provoked to any sort of reprisal by his necessary cool assumption of superiority. She cannot very well help "sassing" him, though she feels that this puts her at a disadvantage, and makes her seem the aggressor.[3]

That confrontation of two American types remained foundational to Howells's fictional vision throughout his career. His perception of what they meant and what they boded for the American future would deepen profoundly and pass through dark changes. But the figure endured — twin stars, the unconventional American type and the conventional, revolving about one another, eclipsing, distorting, perhaps even mutually destroying themselves in collision. Not every Howells novel centered on that figure, but most of them did. And the figure would persist (using publication rather than compositional dates) from *A Chance Acquaintance*, 1873, through *The Vacation of the Kelwyns*, 1920, the year of Howells's death. It provides the great key to most of his fiction.

What Howells meant in *A Chance Acquaintance* by "conventional" Miles Arbuton, hero *manqué*, represents: tastes and convictions that amount to plain snobbery.

They grow in the soil of Europeanized, wealthy, socially exclusive Boston, with its smug pretensions to gentility and superiorities in taste as well as morality. In 1890 Annie R. M. Logan would propose that prior to *A Hazard of New Fortunes* Howells's novels "might be arranged in a series appropriately entitled 'Boston Under the Scalpel,' or 'Boston Torn to Tatters'. . . ."[4] Beyond any shadow of a question, *A Chance Acquaintance* demonstrates that even before Howells had well emerged as *Atlantic* editor he had taken out his scalpel and begun a radical dissection of Boston. He began to serialize the novel, in fact, in the January 1873 issue, the prized New Year's Issue, of the magazine.

The story pioneered in moving "the international theme" entirely to American shores. Now Boston represented wicked Europe and the West republican virtue. Indeed, the whole narrative devotes itself to standing the image of an ideal, patriotic Boston on its head. Consider the explanation of his new "given" that Howells offered to a reader utterly different from Henry James, father Howells. *A Chance Acquaintance* is "decidedly gaining favor. . . . People speak to me of it more than of *Their Wedding Journey*." And then, incredibly in the face of the received wisdom about Howells, "I am glad I have done it for one reason if for no other: it sets me forever outside the rank of mere *culturists*, followers of an elegant literature, and proves that I have sympathy with the true spirit of Democracy. Sometimes I've doubted whether I had, but when I came to look the matter over in writing this story, I doubted no longer. — By the way, do you think that farmer's rebellion against the railroads will spread into Ohio? I'm glad of any union amongst them, for I hope it may lead to some sort of communism and society which is the only thing that can save them from becoming mere peasants."[5] There spoke the spirit of the old

Ashtabula Sentinel, the voice of a radical son to his father and his mentor in radical democracy. Nothing more radical appears even in his Altrurian Romances or his radical essays of the 1890s.

Was Howells always thereafter quite consistent in his faithfulness to radical democratic thought? No, of course not. He was a complicated person who lived sensitively in a complex world that changed rapidly, constantly, massively. Like Emerson, he could take to himself the defense of many-mindedness: "I am always inconsistent, as always knowing there are other moods." But that strand of radically democratic thought and feeling woven into his makeup by his radical education in Ohio never disappeared. It always affected his creative impulse and its figures of expression. It was ineradicable. Though it seemed more prominent at some moments in his career than at others, it never had to be revived. Howells never had to be reconverted — by Tolstoi or anyone else.

Howells imagined the character of Miles Arbuton by homogenizing certain Bostonians he knew with some of his own convictions and fears. He had much more substantial materials to blend into the characters of his "unconventional" Ellisons. Some of that material came right from home — his father's house and his own. Where shall a young novelist with a wife his own age and three younger sisters learn about women? His wife, moreover, was a shrewd observer and a sharp critic of what he read aloud to her soon after writing it. Much of their life together had been spent in foreign residence and travel, and they delighted to watch and talk over the behavior of other people. As Henry Adams had remarked about *Their Wedding Journey*, any author who knew that much about women must have "had feminine aid and counsel. . . ." And yet if Kitty was in certain ways like Elinor and Victoria and Aurelia and Anne, she was quite different from any or all of them.

If you went in a time before the cities, and perhaps between them even now, east along the south coast of Lake Erie from Cleveland to, say, Dunkirk, you crossed three state boundaries: Ohio, Pennsylvania, and New York. Yet the climate, countryside, populations and their culture, and their dominant politics were pretty much all one. An "Eriecreek" might be anywhere in that lacustrine region. It rather resembles Jefferson, Ohio; but so did a hundred other towns. Ellison was a bit like father Howells, or his sons and the sons of Giddings and Wade; but he was something like Garfield or Comly or Mitchell. Like many authors, Howells arrived at characters and settings by blending fictional people out of elements taken from multiple real sources, distilling out characteristics he wanted and "setting" his characters with imaginative ingredients. Nevertheless there remains a distinct savor of Jefferson, Ohio, during the John Brown period about the Ellisons and the village of Eriecreek.

"The Ellisons were a West Virginia family who had wandered up into a corner of Northwestern New York, because Dr. Ellison . . . was too much an abolitionist to live in a slaveholding state with safety to himself or comfort to his neighbors." To his family Ellison had added Kitty, the orphan of his youngest brother, a "country editor" killed "in one of the border feuds" in Bleeding Kansas. In a household of love, Kitty has been educated in the "extreme ideas, tempered with humor" that formed the character of the household. Much associated with abolitionists, they ran a busy station on the Underground Railroad, helping fugitive slaves "over the line" to Canada (p. 6).

Boston, as a result — the Boston of John Quincy Adams and of the Free-Soil party — had become "Dr. Ellison's foible." It was the cradle of liberty and justice. After the Emancipation Proclamation had happily destroyed "Uncle Jack's" usefulness and after the close of the war, the doctor lived "for an ideal Boston" and dreamed of visiting there. It is on the journey to fulfill that cherished dream, taking the steamer down the St. Lawrence and around to Boston, that the "conventional" principle meets its antithesis. Miles and Kitty, rather uncomfortably to both, find themselves engaged in serious courtship with the ultimate object of matrimony.

Not to try tracing the plot, Kitty finds Miles, even when he is doing his best, difficult and puzzling. When he forgets to love her and behaves according to caste, she finds him impossible. And Howells found himself, quite daringly for an author of his first comedy of manners, defying the literary convention of the happy ending. He wrote some revealing speeches and meditations for Kitty:

> " . . . *He* seems to judge people according to their origin and locality and calling, and to believe that all refinement must come from just such training and circumstances as his own. . . . He tramples upon all that I have been taught to believe; and though I cling the closer to my idols, I can't help, now and then, trying myself by his criterions; and then I find myself wanting in every civilized trait, and my whole life coarse and poor, and all my associations hopelessly degraded. I think his ideas are hard and narrow, and I believe that even my little experience would prove them false; but then, they are his, and I can't reconcile them with what I see is good in him." (144)

And again,

> . . . She was aware that there had been gradually rising in her mind an image of Boston, different alike from the holy place of her childhood, the sacred city of the anti-slavery heroes and martyrs, and from the jesting, easy, sympathetic

Boston of Mr. and Mrs. March.[6] This new Boston with which
Mr. Arbuton inspired her was a Boston of mysterious pre-
judices and lofty reservations; a Boston of high and difficult
tastes, that found its social ideal in the Old World, and that
shrank from contact with the reality of this; a Boston as alien
as Europe to her simple experiences, and that seemed to be
proud only of the things that were unlike other American
things; a Boston that would rather perish by fire and sword
than be suspected of vulgarity; a critical, fastidious, and
reluctant Boston, dissatisfied with the rest of the hemi-
sphere, and gelidly self-satisfied. (152–53)

Then, at last, to Arbuton himself:

> "I'm afraid I can't enter into your feelings. I wasn't taught to
> respect the idea of a gentleman very much. I've often heard
> my uncle say that, at the best, it was a poor excuse for not
> being just honest and just brave and just kind, and a false
> pretense of being something more. I believe, if I were a man,
> I shouldn't want to be a gentleman." (166)

The comedy in the working out, then, proves to be not
so much a comedy of manners as an ironic study in
clashing values. Out of the conflict, the "unconventional," the real, the common, the democratic, and at the
final depth the radically democratic, end in triumph. It is
a victory with losses—Arbuton ends crushed and Kitty
sorely hurt by the conflict. But over it, from the earliest
beginnings, there presides the vivid figure of "one aboli-
tion visitor" to the Ellisons' home during Kitty's childhood "of whom none of them made fun, but treated with
a serious distinction and regard."

> —An old man with a high, narrow forehead, and thereon a
> thick upright growth of gray hair; who looked at her from
> under bushy brows with eyes as of blue flame, and took her
> on his knee one night and sang to her "Blow ye the trumpet,
> blow!" He and her uncle had been talking of some indefin-
> ite, far-off place that they called Boston, in terms that com-

mended it to her childish apprehension as very little less holy
than Jerusalem, and as the home of all the good and great
people outside of Palestine. (6)

It is "Old Brown" to the life.

Had John Brown visited in the Howells household?
Most unlikely; it is also the wrong question. It misses the
point of the vignette. For the point is that over the launch-
ing of Howells's true career as a novelist there presided a
mythic figure. Over the initiation of his lifelong explora-
tion of his basic and tropological figure of American
fiction, the thematic on which the bulk of his work centers, Howells set the image of the martyr for liberty, for
radical democracy. John Brown stepped out of Howells's
ground in Ohio for one moment of one pivotal book.
Briefly but vividly John Brown becomes something like a
domestic *lars* or patron saint of radical democracy in an
American household devoted to that American best
which belongs to the common people at their best. He
sits with a child on his knee and sings John Brown's
favorite hymn, "Blow ye the trumpet, blow!" And everything unworthy in America goes down before him.

NOTES

1. *Radical/Radicalism.* The use of such words involves many risks of misunderstanding and predilection in a reader's mind. They have been used so often and in such widely variant patterns of signification, that one risks the danger of cliché: the useless smudge imprinted by the piece of type too battered by wear to cut its sign legibly. They stir up the lees of prejudice, pro or con, in some minds. Nevertheless, they were current a century and a third ago. They are current today—and what words replace them? *Radix malorum est cupiditas*, Chaucer's Pardoner droned more than five hundred years ago. I try, then, to use the terms neutrally, according to common informed usage. A "radical" seeks to extirpate or to reform what he thinks evil by attacking at the roots. "Radicalism" I take to be the habit of mind or temperament or intellectual behavior that favors radical belief and radical action.

2. *Treason.* Legally, which is to say learnedly and technically, "treason" has a complex history. John Brown and his captured men were mostly tried and hanged for treason against the Commonwealth of Virginia. Copeland and Green, being black and "not" citizens, were hanged for rebellion and murder. They might all equally well have been tried, convicted, and hanged for treason against the United States of America. At that moment just before the Civil War, the relations of the several sovereign states to the United States were uniquely delicate. Thence came John Brown's terrorist opportunity to destabilize them. Whether Ashtabula County's escapees from the Harper's Ferry raid were technically guilty of Brown's crimes, or whether the Black String or others who gave "aid and comfort" to the fugitives were rightfully liable to the penalties of the law are moot questions. Were they liable to indictment for treason, or "constructive treason," for being accessories to such crimes? They thought it best to shelter themselves in safe places until the danger blew over, and they may well have been wise.

I am deeply grateful to Professor A. Kenneth Pye of the Duke University Law School for guidance in the legal literature. Especially useful have been the series in *American State Trials*, ed. John D. Lawson. (St. Louis: F. H. Thomas, 1916). Vol. 6 includes "The Trial of John Brown . . ." (700); "The Trial of Edwin Coppoc . . ." (806); "The Trial of John Anthony Copeland and Shields Green . . ." (809); and "The Trial of John E. Cook . . ." (814). Also, the three-part essay by Willard Hurst in the *Harvard Law Review* 58 (1944–45). The parts appear as "I. Treason Down to the Constitution," (December 1944), pp. 226–72; "II. The Constitution," (February 1945), pp. 395–444; and "III. Under the Constitution." (July 1945), pp. 806–57.

3. *Other Sources.* Among the background studies important to me here have been R. Carlyle Buley, *The Old Northwest: Pioneer Period, 1815–1840.* 2 vols. (Bloomington: Indiana University Press, 1950); and Allan Nevins, *Ordeal of the Union,* I: *Fruits of Manifest Destiny, 1842–1852* (New York: Scribner's, 1947); II. *A House Dividing, 1852–1857* (New York: Scribner's, 1947). Also, Mary Land, "John Brown's Ohio Environment," *OSAHQ,* January 1948.

4. *Howells Sources.* At present the most useful resources for the study of Howells are materials mostly published during the past twenty years or so. Knowledge of them is indispensable to approaching the massive archival materials not yet edited.

See first: William M. Gibson and George Arms, *A Bibliography of William Dean Howells* (New York: New York Public Library, 1948). Also *Interviews with William Dean Howells,* ed. Ulrich Halfmann (Arlington: University of Texas at Arlington, 1973). *W. D. Howells as Critic,* ed. Edwin H. Cady (London: Routledge & Kegan Paul, 1973). *Published Comment on William Dean Howells through 1920,* ed. Clayton L. Eichelberger (Boston: G. K. Hall, 1976). And "A Bibliography of Writing about William Dean Howells. Part Two: 1920-Present," ed. Stanley P. Anderson, *American Literary Realism, 1870–1910,* Special Number 1969.

Though no intensive study of Howells's years in Ohio has yet appeared, biographical accounts may be found in Edwin H. Cady, *The Road to Realism: The Early Years, 1837–1885, of William Dean Howells* (Syracuse: Syracuse University Press, 1956); and Kenneth S. Lynn, *William Dean Howells: An American Life* (New York: Harcourt Brace Jovanovich, 1971).

A trove of treasure that scholars may be long in exhausting lies in two series that emanate from the Howells Center, Indiana University. One, best called the "Indiana Edition," has edited a number of fundamental texts according to admirable standards. Edited by many hands in a project ongoing since 1968, each volume carries in its several sections of introduction and explanatory notes information that is often of major interest to the biographer, the bibliographer, or the literary historian. Properly introduced, the "Indiana Edition" is A Selected Edition of W. D. Howells (Bloomington: Indiana University Press). Each separate volume requires its own entry; and the one most important to the student of Howells in Ohio is W. D. Howells, *Years of My Youth and Three Other Essays,* ed. David J. Nordloh, Indiana Edition, Vol. 29 (Bloomington: Indiana University Press, 1975).

The second series from the Howells Center has a different publisher and may best be called "Letters" for short. The biographical "Introductions" and the annotations to letters are particularly valuable. The volume of *Letters* most applicable to the study of Howells in Ohio is W. D. Howells, *Selected Letters, Vol. 1:*

1852–1872. It is edited and annotated by George Arms, Richard H. Ballinger, Christoph K. Lohmann, and John K. Reeves; with Don L. Cook, in addition to Lohmann and Nordloh, as textual editors (Boston: Twayne, 1979). Succeeding volumes are: 2: *1873–1881* (1979); 3: *1882–1891* (1980); 4: *1892–1901* (1981); 5: *1902–1911* (1983); and 6: *1912–1920* (1983). Though the *Letters* considerably expand and occasionally correct, they do not supersede Mildred Howells, *Life in Letters of William Dean Howells*, 2 vols. (New York: Doubleday, Doran, 1928); and *Mark Twain–Howells Letters*, ed. Henry Nash Smith and William M. Gibson. 2 vols. (Cambridge: Harvard University Press, 1960). Of something like equal value with the foregoing are: *The Complete Plays of W. D. Howells*, ed. Walter J. Meserve (New York: New York University Press, 1960); and *Critical Essays on W. D. Howells*, ed. Edwin H. and Norma W. Cady (Boston: G. K. Hall, 1983).

5. *John Brown Sources*. The "givens" of this book preclude an effort to sift through the mountain of John Brown resources. Aside from works cited in the References, I found the following to be particularly interesting and informative: James Redpath, *Echoes of Harper's Ferry* (Boston: Thayer and Eldridge, 1860); Richard J. Hinton, *John Brown and His Men* (London: Funk and Wagnalls, 1894; repr. New York: Arno Press, 1968); Stephen B. Oates, *To Purge This Land with Blood: A Biography of John Brown* (New York: Harper & Row, 1970); Jules Abels, *Man on Fire: John Brown and the Cause of Liberty* (New York: Macmillan, 1971); Benjamin Quarles, ed., *Blacks on John Brown* (Urbana: University of Illinois Press, 1972); Jeffrey Rossbach, *Ambivalent Conspirators: John Brown, the Secret Six, and a Theory of Slave Violence* (Philadelphia: University of Pennsylvania Press, 1982).

6. *In Brief: Antislavery Politics*. Since several readers have asked for a brief overview of the antislavery politics of the period, I hope the following will suffice. The story of the 1850s really begins with the Whig victory of Zachary Taylor over Lewis Cass. The election hinged on the success of a coalition of Democratic "Barnburners," "Conscience Whigs," and the new Free-Soil party in carrying swing states away from Cass. After Taylor's death in 1850, Millard Fillmore as a Whig president signed the Compromise of 1850 and, apparently simultaneously, the death warrant of the Whig party. By 1860, a wholly new party, the Republican, elected Abraham Lincoln.

The intervening years were chaotic. Conscience Whigs, antislavery, went off to join the Free-Soil party, which disappeared into the Republican party when it was organized in 1854. "Barnburner," or Independent, Democrats, also antislavery, took roughly the same route. Once established, the Republicans tended to show stress lines of belief that, among other sources, reflected the diverse origins of the group. Very roughly speaking, the most significant divisions were three. The mass divided between the Regular, or Unionist, Republicans, for whom the preservation of the Union was a paramount concern. On the other side stood the Radical Republicans, for whom the destruction of slavery was paramount. The Radicals, again, inclined to split into gradualists of various sorts who wished to end slavery peacefully and over a period of time – Antislavery men; and those who stood on the other side, who would take the most aggressive, immediate, and if necessary violent means to sweep away slavery – the Abolitionists.

Very important in defining and agitating public opinion were three factors. The first of those was the Compromise of 1850. With what were regarded as its coercive provisions against conscientious antislavery folk, the Fugitive Slave Law of 1850 raised crises of conscience in citizens who had been less than militant before: "I will not obey it, by God" swore even Waldo Emerson. Confrontation, agitation, civil disobedience, and incivil violence increased almost geometrically. The fiery focus, the great rehearsal for the Civil War, centered in "Bleeding Kansas." Guerrilla war, the training ground for John Brown and his men, ebbed and flowed in Kansas during its border war (1854–56). Its progress toward temporary chaos was speeded by the genius for combined indecisiveness, irresponsibility, imperception, and cowardice that has made the name of James Buchanan notorious.

In the campaign of 1856, Buchanan beat John C. Frémont, first Republican nominee, with Millard Fillmore, former Whig, perhaps drawing off the swing votes for Frémont with his maverick "'Know-Nothing' Party." In 1860 there were no less than four candidates: Stephen A. Douglas, Democrat; John G. Breckenridge, proslavery Democrat; John Bell, Constitutional Union (mainly Old Whig); and Abraham Lincoln, Republican. There are analysts who believe that John Brown's act at Harpers Ferry so infuriated and indurated southern Democrats that, had it not happened, there would have been no Democratic split and Douglas would have won.

7. *What Happened at Harpers Ferry.* Courteous readers, whose judgment I respect, have severally asked: "But just what happened at Harpers Ferry?" I stand far from professional expertise about John Brown, but I will try to take a bird's-eye point of view and survey the main points of the Harpers Ferry raid. I think it helps to understand Brown's intent: he meant to seize control of the stands of infantry arms in the Unites States Arsenal at Harpers Ferry. For a few shocking hours, he succeeded. With the arsenal's weapons, he meant to arm a multitude of militant black slaves believed to be eager to leap to the opportunity. With that Libera-

tion Army so gathered, he meant to crush the organized system of slavery, even if he had to fight a mass guerrilla war from the mountains. There turned out to be no substance to his dream of a potential army: he took the arms, but nobody came in to catch them up and join him in the fight.

The details are therefore commonplace and sometimes sordid. Leaving three men to guard his armory, Brown set out with eighteen men and one wagon from a "hideout" just across the Maryland line on the night of 16 October 1859. He promptly captured sleepy, ill-secured Harpers Ferry, arsenal and all. He distributed details from his little squad about the town and at certain strategic points outside it, the posts probably calculated to serve the expected influx of black soldiers. For some hours he shocked the town, the Commonwealth of Virginia, and the federal govenment out of their wits. But there was no influx of slave fighting men. He brooded away Monday morning, 17 October, refusing to escape by the open road to the hills, while resistance began to thicken around him.

Harpers Ferry citizens, the Virginia militia, and even President Buchanan began to recover. The president found that he had a couple of platoons of U.S. Marines combat-ready in Washington. He put Robert E. Lee in command, J. E. B. Stuart second, and dispatched them by rail to Harpers Ferry. Meanwhile, Virginians had begun to swarm on the surrounding hills and around the town, sharpshooting down Captain Brown's little parties. Finally, the casualties would be: killed, Harpers Ferry citizens, four; Brown's men (mostly experienced Kansas guerrilla fighters), ten. Brown withdrew, with hostages he had taken and the remnant of his men, to the enginehouse of the arsenal.

On Tuesday morning, early, the marines demanded Brown's instant, unconditional surrender. Brown replied that he wished to parley. Stuart led an immediate storming-party, burst into the enginehouse, and killed or wounded most of Brown's remaining men. Brown surrendered with saber wounds in his head and side. After that, the remaining action became war by other means: legal process, executions, and propaganda.

REFERENCES

CHAPTER ONE

1. W. D. Howells, *Selected Letters*, (hereafter *Letters*, with volume number), *Volume I, 1852–1872*, ed. George Arms and others (Boston: Twayne, 1979), pp. 54–55.

2. *Recollections of Life in Ohio from 1813 to 1840* (Cincinnati: Robert Clarke, 1895).

3. In addition to *Recollections*, see Annette Walsh, "Three Anti-Slavery Newspapers prior to 1823," *Ohio History* 31 (1922): 172–217.

4. Arthur E. Bestor, Jr., *Backwoods Utopias* (Philadelphia: University of Pennsylvania Press, 1950).

5. W. D. Howells, *Years of My Youth*, Indiana Edition (Bloomington: Indiana University Press, 1975), p. 36.

CHAPTER TWO

1. Quoted from George W. Julian, *The Life of Joshua R. Giddings* (Chicago: McClurg. 1892), pp. 168–70.

2. *Report: The Select Committee of the Senate appointed to inquire into the late invasion and seizure of the public property at Harper's Ferry* . . . pp. 147–49. Rep. Com. No. 278. 36th Cong. 1st Sess. By special order of the Senate on 21 June 1860, it was resolved that an edition of 20,000 copies of the report be published "for the use of the Senate." The document is ordinarily referred to as the "Mason Committee Report."

3. Lawson, 6: 713 (see "Notes: 2, 'Treason' ").

4. Lawson, 6: 834–48.

5. William W. Williams et al., *History of Ashtabula County, Ohio: With Illustrations and Biographical Sketches of Its Pioneers and Most Prominent Men* (Philadelphia: Williams Bros., 1878).

6. Williams, p. 35.

CHAPTER THREE

1. *Letters*, 1:48–49.

2. *John Brown and Ashtabula County*. By Chet [Chester A.] Lampson (Jefferson, O.: Jefferson *Gazette*, 1955).

3. Joseph A. Howells to Richard J. Hinton, 30 November 1895, Hinton Collection, University of Kansas, Lawrence.

CHAPTER FOUR

1. The standard authority appears still to be Albert Bushnell Hart, *Salmon Portland Chase*, (Boston: Houghton, Mifflin, 1899).

2. See esp. *Life of Abraham Lincoln by W. D. Howells*, Facsimile, Ed. with introduction and published by Abraham Lincoln Association, Springfield, Ill., 1938; Reprinted *in toto* with Introduction by Clyde C. Walton (Bloomington: Indiana University Press, 1960).

3. *The Works of James Russell Lowell*, Vol. 7, Standard Library Edition (Boston: Houghton Mifflin, 1890), p. 72.

4. Martin Duberman, *James Russell Lowell* (Boston: Houghton, Mifflin, 1965), pp. 174–77.

5. *Letters*, 1:83.

6. *Literary Friends and Acquaintance*, Indiana Edition (Bloomington: Indiana University Press, 1968), p. 72. See also H. L. Trefousse, *Benjamin Franklin Wade: Radical Republican from Ohio* (New York: Twayne, 1963).

CHAPTER FIVE

1. *Life in Letters*, 2:243–44.

2. "The Rambler," *Book Buyer* n.s. 14 (July 1897): 559.

3. 10 March 1873, *Letters*, 2:17.

4. "Mr. Howells's Latest Novel," *Nation* 50 (5 June 1890): 454.

5. 20 April 1873, *Letters*, 2:24.

6. Of *Their Wedding Journey* (though Basil March is a western man).

INDEX

Adams, Charles Francis, 23
Adams, Henry, 100
Adams, John, 88
Adams, John Quincy, 21, 22–23, 101
American Revolution, 20, 23, 41, 88–89
Andover, Ohio, 26, 31, 42, 43, 44, 50, 56–57, 73
Antislavery cause and Abolitionism, 8–9, 13, 17–18, 32–35, 68, 81, 89, 90, 107–8
Arms, George, 67
Articles of Confederation, 19
Ashtabula County, Ohio, 3–4, 5, 17–18, 36, 39–40, 41–45, 51, 53, 54, 56, 57, 59, 67, 72–73, 105
Ashtabula Sentinel, 18, 20, 22, 34, 38, 41–42, 47–62, 64, 67, 89, 100
Atlantic Monthly, 65, 67, 68, 71, 74, 79, 80–81, 82, 93, 94, 95, 96, 97, 99
Aveling, Elinor Marx, 5

"Barnburners," 107
Bell, John, 61, 108
Bestor, Arthur, Jr., 12
Blackstone, 27
Black String, the, 48, 49, 50, 51, 53–56, 58, 61, 63, 105
Blackstring Band, the, 43, 57
Blackwoods Quarterly, 27
Boston, Mass., 40, 69, 71, 73, 79–80, 81, 97, 99–104
Breckenridge, John G., 61, 108
Brown, John, 3, 5, 6, 28, 29–33, 34–37, 38–45, 47–48, 51, 53, 61, 63, 65, 67–68, 68, 69, 70, 71, 72, 74, 80–81, 92, 101, 103–4, 105, 108–9
Brown, John, Jr., 34, 42, 44, 48–49, 49–50, 51, 52, 61, 73
Brown, Owen, 51, 52, 60
Bryant, William Cullen, 88
Buchanan, James, 108, 209

Cahan, Abraham, 5
Calhoun, John C., 24
Cass, Lewis, 107

Chase, Kate, 69
Chase, Salmon P., 17, 22, 23–24, 47, 68, 68–69, 82, 83
Chatham, Ontario, 41
Cherry Valley, Ohio, 44
Chesnutt, Charles W., 5
Chicago Haymarket Anarchists, 3, 5, 6
Cincinnati, Ohio, 10, 11, 17, 64, 82
Cincinnati Gazette, 64, 72, 73, 90
Civil War, 10, 89–90, 91, 95, 105, 108
Clarke, James Freeman, 68
Clay, Henry, 9
Clemens, Samuel L., 79, 87, 89
Cleveland, Ohio, 31, 36, 64, 73, 101
Cleveland Plain Dealer, 54, 57, 58, 60
Coggeshall, William T., 70, 73
Cole, Thomas, 88–89
Coleman, John A., 96
Columbus, Ohio, 5, 17, 47, 64, 69, 71, 72, 73, 81–82, 92
Comly, James M., 90, 101
Compromise of 1850, 107, 108
Conneaut, Ohio, 43
Connecticut, 19–20
Conscience Whigs, 17, 23–24, 107
Conway, Moncure D., 86
Cook, John E., 36–37
Cooke, Henry, 68, 69, 81–82
Copeland, John A., 105
Coppoc, Barclay, 51, 52, 60, 61, 72–73
Crane, Stephen, 5, 79
Crosby, Ernest, 5

Dayton, Ohio, 14–16, 25
Dayton Transcript, 14–16, 64
Democratic party, 8, 13, 23, 33–34, 35, 68, 107–8
Don Quixote, 15
Dorset, Ohio, 42, 43, 44, 49, 50, 56, 73
Douglas, Stephen A., 61, 63, 108
Douglass, Frederick, 39
Dunbar, Paul Lawrence, 5
Dunkirk, N.Y., 101

Dubois, W. E. B., 5
Dwight, Timothy, 20

Edinburgh Review, 27
Emancipation Proclamation, 70, 90, 102
Emerson, Ralph Waldo, 81, 89, 100, 108
Eureka Mills, Ohio, 16–18, 25, 66

Fabian Socialists, 5
Fields, James T., 80, 81, 93, 97
Fillmore, Millard, 107, 108
Follett and Foster, 69, 70, 71, 73
Fourier, Charles, 12
Free-Soil Movement, 13, 17, 22–23, 69, 89, 101, 107
Frémont, John C., 108
Freneau, Philip, 88
Freud, Sigmund, 66
Freyer, E. L., 3–5, 50, 72
Fugitive Slave Law, 28, 108

Garfield, James A., 82, 90, 101
Garibaldi, Giuseppe, 85, 86
Garland, Hamlin, 5
Garrison, William Lloyd, 67
Gibson, William M., 67
Giddings, Joshua R., 21–24, 25, 28–35, 36, 37, 38, 39, 41, 43, 47–49, 52, 59, 63, 68, 80, 83, 101
Gilded Age, 91–93
Godkin, E. L., 90, 91–93
Gompers, Samuel, 5
Grant, Ulysses S., 60, 94
Green, Shields, 105

Hamilton, Ohio, 9–13, 14, 25
Hamilton Intelligencer, 9–13, 14, 60
Hapsburg Empire, 85–88
Harpers Ferry, Va., 3, 28, 35–36, 37, 39–40, 43, 44–45, 47, 48, 57, 61, 69, 105, 108, 108–9
Harvard College, 22, 25
Hay, John, 82
Hayes, Rutherford B., 17, 82, 90
Hazlett, Albert, 51, 52
Heine, Heinrich, 65–67, 92
Hendry, William, 3–4
Higginson, Thomas W., 81, 96
Hillquit, Morris, 5
Hinton, Richard, 3, 37, 41, 57, 63

Holmes, Oliver Wendell, 80–81, 93, 97
Howells, Ann Thomas, 7–8
Howells, Israel, 16–17
Howells, Joseph (1783–1858), 7, 16
Howells, Joseph A., 10, 12, 57–61
Howells, Mary Dean, 11, 13–14, 17, 59
Howells, William Cooper, 7–18, 48–49, 50, 51, 51–52, 58, 61, 63, 68, 69, 82–83, 92, 99, 101
Howells, William Dean, writings: *A Boy's Town*, 9–10; *A Chance Acquaintance*, 62, 97–104; *A Hazard of New Fortunes*, 99; "Andenken," 65–67; "Gerrit Smith," 48, 67; "Glimpses of Summer Travel," 73; *Italian Journeys*, 94; "Letters from the Country," 22–23; *Lives and Speeches of Abraham Lincoln and Hannibal Hamlin*, 65, 69–71; *My Literary Passions*, 27–28; "Old Brown," 3, 48, 67; *Poems of Two Friends*, 51, 69; *Sketch of the Life and Character of Rutherford B. Hayes*, 65; *Stops of Various Quills*, 64; *Suburban Sketches*, 94; "The Country Printer," 25; "The Editor's Study," 95; "The Independent Candidate," 64–65; "The Pilot's Story," 68, 73–79, 81, 84; *The Vacation of the Kelwyns*, 98; *The World of Chance*, 62; *Their Wedding Journey*, 95, 97, 99, 100; *Venetian Life*, 86–88, 89, 94
Hudson, Ohio, 40

Imperialism, 5, 85–88, 89, 89–90
Independent Sons of Liberty, 50
Irving, Washington, 72, 84

Jackson, Andrew, 83
James, Henry, 91, 97–98
Jefferson Gazette, 54, 58
Jefferson, Ohio, 14, 15, 18, 21, 25–27, 28, 29, 33, 39, 47, 49, 50, 60, 72, 92, 101
Jefferson, Thomas, 88
Johnson, Andrew, 94
Johnson, M., 49–50

Kagi, John Henri, 44
Kansas, 26, 28, 30, 39, 40, 41, 48–49, 108
Knights of the Golden Circle, 34, 35

Lake Erie, 19, 20, 43, 101
Lampson, Chester A., 54–58
Lee, Robert E., 109
Liberty party, 23
Lincoln, Abraham, 13, 52, 53, 61, 63, 68, 69–71, 73, 81, 82, 83, 89, 107, 108
Lloyd, Henry Demarest, 91
Logan, Annie R. M., 99
London Quarterly, 27
Lowell, James Russell, 20, 65, 67, 79–81, 90, 97

Maryland, 41, 44, 49, 109
Mason, James M., 28–33, 37, 43
Mason Committee, 28–33, 34, 38, 43, 51, 61, 67
Massachusetts, 19, 23, 26
Mead, Elinor, 82, 100–101
Melville, Herman, 83–84, 88–89
Merriam, Francis J., 51, 52, 60, 61
Methodism, 8
Mexican War, 13, 19
Mitchell, John G., 90, 101

Nast, Thomas, 59
Nation, the, 90–93
National Association for the Advancement of Colored People, 5
New York, 19, 101
New York City, 64, 71, 81, 90–93
New York Times, 90
New York World, 82
Niagara Falls, 73, 95
Nicolay, John G., 82
North British Quarterly, 27
North Elba, N.Y., 41
Norton, Charles Eliot, 90

Ohio, 18, 19, 24, 101
Ohio State Journal, 17, 47, 64, 68, 69, 72–73, 81–82, 89
Owen, Robert, 8, 16

Paine, Thomas, 8
Painesville, Ohio, 31

Palfrey, Francis, 23
Papal States, 85
Parker, Theodore, 81
Peace Democrats, 13, 33–34, 35
Pennsylvania, 19, 43, 101
Perry, Benjamin, 58
Phillips, Wendell, 37, 81
Pittsburgh, Pa., 8
Pymatuning Swamp, 43

Quakers and Quakerism, 7–8, 13, 34–35, 40–41

"Radical/Radicalism," 105
Radical Republicans, 47, 63, 69, 70, 86, 89, 90, 108
Realf, Richard, 3, 51
Redpath, James, 3, 48, 51, 61, 63, 67–68, 69
Reid, Whitelaw, 90
Republican party, 13, 59–60, 60–61, 68, 80, 82, 89, 95, 107–8
Retina, the, 10–12
Ruffin, Edmund, 69

St. Louis, Mo., 8
Sarpi, Paolo, 86–88
Saturday Press, 71, 80, 82
"Secret Six, The," 40, 81
Seward, William H., 37
Smith, Gerrit, 34, 41
Socialism, 8, 9, 11–12, 15
Sons of Liberty, 42
Spartacus, 43
Springdale, Iowa, 40–41, 73
Springfield, Ill., 70, 73
Steubenville, Ohio, 8, 36
Stevens, Aaron, 35, 44, 51, 52
Stuart, J. E. B., 109
Sumner, Charles, 23, 68–69
Swedenborg and Swedenborgianism, 9, 10–12

Taft, William Howard, 84
Taylor, Zachary, 13, 107
Territorial Ordinances, 19
Thoreau, Henry D., 47, 81
Ticknor, Howard M., 68, 79, 81
Tidd, Charles P., 52, 60, 61
Tolstoi, Leo, 5, 100
"Treason," 105–6
Trevelyan, George Otto, 85

Underground Railroad, 33, 35, 101
Unionism, 70, 89–90, 91, 108
Utopianism, 16–17

Vallandigham, Clement, 35–37, 38
Venice, 82, 83, 84, 85–90, 92–93
Virginia, 19, 29, 37, 49–50, 51, 69, 105, 109
Voorhees, Daniel W., 36–37

Wade, Benjamin F., 22, 23–24, 25–27, 41, 42, 59, 68, 82, 83, 101
Wade, Decius, 26
Wales, 7, 16
War of 1812, 8, 21
Washington, D.C., 49, 82–84
Washington, George, 88

Weld, Theodore, 24
West Andover, Ohio, 43, 44, 49
West Virginia, 101
Western Reserve, the, 4, 17–45, 53, 54
Westminster Quarterly, 27
Wheeling, Va., 8, 36
Whig party, 9–13, 14, 17, 23–24, 68, 107
Whitman, Walt, 92, 93, 94–95
Whittier, John Greenleaf, 67
Wilberforce University, 61
Williams, William W., 43–44, 49, 53–54, 56, 57, 58
Women's rights, 5, 24, 96
Wright, Fanny, 8

Xenia, Ohio, 16